RED IS FOR ROSES

A Cold War Memoir

The Reunion of a Family

Lisa Ann Varco and
Vanya Nikolova Pirincheva-Toteva
with Natasha Fernando

Red Is for Roses
Copyright © 2019 by Lisa Ann Varco and Vanya Nikolova Pirincheva-Toteva

Published by Lisa Ann Varco, Buffalo, New York
Cover and Interior Design by Lisa Ann Varco

Printed by IngramSpark

Varco, Lisa, 2019-
Red Is for Roses: A Cold War Memoir
ISBN Number: 978-1-7330995-0-9
Ebook ISBN: 978-1-7330995-1-6

Reach us on the Internet: www.redisforroses.com

DEDICATION

RANGEL
my great-nephew, I am blessed to have you in my life.
You were that missing link I needed.

KYLE
my son, the reason for the book,
a legacy for the future generations, my pride and joy.

ATANAS RANGELOV PIRINCHEV
my dad whose hope helped him to survive a difficult life.
We have not forgotten.

ACKNOWLEDGMENTS

TOM

First and foremost, thank you to my husband, Tom, who has stood by me through everything. Without your support, encouragement and love, this book would not have been possible. You prompted me to write and provided the resources necessary to make it happen. You loved me even when I made excuses as to why I couldn't finish the project. You're my biggest fan. I love you.

VANYA

Thank you to my niece, Vanya Nikolova Pirincheva-Toteva, who embraced me like a sister and contributed to the writing of this book. You added the special details about our family. Without your tenacity and planning, this book would not have been possible.
I love you.

RUTH

To my long-time friend, Ruth, thank you for your friendship and incredible organizational and editing skills. You lived the last steps of the book with me helping me gather my thoughts together and finalize the project.

LINDA

Thank you to my friend and prayer partner, Linda, who agreed with me in prayer that Thanksgiving Day.
Prayer changes everything!

HELGA

Thank you to Helga for your dear friendship and help in times of need. Your Bulgarian translation skills helped to bridge the communication gap. You are a blessing!

MY AMERICAN FAMILY

Thank you to my American family: mother, brother and sister for always being here for me through it all even when you didn't know the whole story. You are my family and I love you. Thank you to my mom's sisters and brothers who helped me remember my dad.

MY BULGARIAN FAMILY
Thank you to my Bulgarian family, their spouses and friends who hosted, chauffeured, fed and translated for us while on our trip to a far land. You are my heroes.

DON
Thank you to Don for befriending my dad.

BOB SIMON
Thank you to Bob Simon for your selflessness in sponsoring my dad and so many others.

PROFESSOR VILLI LILKOV AND HRISTO HRISTOV
Although not involved in this project, I would like to thank the authors of *Former People* Prof. Villi Lilkov and Hristo Hristov. Please know I am thankful for your work in reconciling stories similar to our own in Bulgaria. For this reason, we appreciate that our story does not stand alone.

NATASHA FERNANDO
A special thank you to my editor and fellow Act One Alumni, Natasha Fernando, for your God-given talent in structuring my story and your words of wisdom in the writing business. I look forward to continuing our writing relationship.
Every time we Skyped, God showed up!

MARIYA NIKOLOVA
Bravo to my Bulgarian translator, Mariya Nikolova, who not only translated this book into Bulgarian but also helped edit my English version. Thank you for a job well done!

OISHEI CHILDREN'S HOSPITAL OF BUFFALO
Thank you to the staff of the former Women & Children's Hospital of Buffalo for taking care of me for three months in 1967. Without your expertise, I would not be here to tell the story.

JESUS
Thank you, Jesus! Without your sacrifice on the cross, this story of redemption wouldn't be worth telling

CONTENTS

INTRODUCTION

Long ago, Bulgaria was home to ancient empires such as the Thracians and Romans. As a military force under Philip II of Macedon and a playground for Alexander the Great, she forgot her strength and beauty. As a stomping ground for the Ottoman-Turks, she forgot her worth. As a friend to the Soviets, she gave up her sovereignty. Besides, like many other countries, she was already worn down by the Balkan and two world wars. Soldiers are never just soldiers, they are husbands, fathers, sons, and brothers. When these men became casualties, families were irretrievably decimated.

As if the world wars were not enough, the Balkans lost thousands more during the Cold War. The women and children left behind including dad's own wife and children were vulnerable to the tortures of the Communist regime. Neighbors turned against neighbors and friends against friends. Even family members turned against their own.

The Bulgarians who allowed the Communism to creep in were not a weak class of people. Their ancestors inhabited that part of the world for thousands of years. When hardship came, they faced it head on, embracing it as just another challenge. If 500 years of Ottoman torture and oppression taught them anything it was to be true to themselves. They became survivors with an autonomy of their own while merging into the society of their conquerors. A people steeped in rich traditions and Bulgarian Orthodox Christianity, they held firm to their beliefs even when it was not safe to do so.

Even today in towns such as Smolyan, the Bulgarians hold no resentment and live side by side with their Muslim neighbors. In fact, it is very apt that the 2019 European Capital of Culture is Plovdiv, or rather styled as pLOVEdiv in the advertising campaign. Indeed, to love one another takes strength and as I said, the Bulgarians are not a weak people.

The commandment, as it is written in the scripture:

And you shall love the Lord your God with all your heart, with all your soul, with all your mind, and with all your strength. This is the first commandment. And the second, like it, is this: 'You shall love your neighbor as yourself.' There is no other commandment greater than these." *(Mark 12:31).*

This was my dad's philosophy. Unfortunately, the second part of this scripture, got him into trouble with man but not with God.

We learned about the Cold War with the Cuban Missile Crisis which was not far off the Florida coast. The Sunshine State was still very far from Buffalo, New York where I grew up. In the 1970's, the air raid drills that forced us to take cover under our desks were more of a break from lessons - not too effective in helping us comprehend any dangers.

In 11th grade, our required English reading was George Orwell's *1984*. After reading it, the theme of the book haunted me for years. The dangers of Communism seemed like something we should never allow to occur. Little did I know this Communism had already hit home in the past to a family I would eventually meet at a God-appointed time in the future.

PART I

LIFE AS A BULGARIAN

Chapter 1. The Land Between Two Rivers

A round 1917, my father became an orphan and his mother a widow after my grandfather was killed in World War I. I can only imagine her sorrow. My grandmother allowed her brother and sister-in-law, who were barren, to adopt my dad. His birth mother remarried after the war and started a new life without him. Upon dad's arrival, there was a special blessing on the family of Kiro and Luba and their house became more of a home. He was well cared for by his loving aunt and uncle, his new parents.

Between 1930 and 1944, Grandfather Kiro introduced an irrigation system with a gasoline motor for plantations. With this system they were able to irrigate the lands between the Maritsa and Chai Rivers. They were convinced that their success stemmed not only from the invention but also from the workers they employed. To run a successful business like this was a team effort and they cared for their employees as if they were their own children. As the workers grew, so did the business.

Kiro and Luba set aside a small tract of land for each of their workers in the village and assisted them with a home. An honorable couple, they stepped in as best man and matron of honor at their weddings. As an extension of their own family, seven workers in all, Grandma Luba turned her house into a true Abraham's home, complete with many grandchildren who visited often.

My dad married Ruska who gave birth to three daughters and one son. Grandma Luba looked forward to the summers after the grandchildren were born and loaded her cart with food. With the grandkids in tow, along with livestock and chickens, she harnessed the horses and took them to Velingrad where they rented a vacation home all summer long. Ruska was not afraid to work hard and oversaw the workers. Making them meals of *tarator* soup with garlic cloves and cucumbers, she took soup and fresh bread to the workers in the fields even arriving home late in the evening. Life in those days was good and they appreciated all the blessings of God.

My dad and grandfather were busy travelling to and from work, and they often invited businessmen or technicians to the home to talk about topics such as diesel motors. Luba, a very hospitable woman was always prepared with baked cookies and *banitza*, a traditional baked flaky pastry, for their guests.

Grandfather Kiro was an entrepreneur, the first retailer of strawberries in the area. Here they built a small manufacturing plant. The men had high hopes of expanding their facility with the agricultural land available. The cultivated strawberry plants thrived. At harvest time, the production plant was busy where the workers handled the fragile fruits. There in the plant, the strawberries were washed and specially treated before being loaded and packed into wooden barrels. They exported strawberry pulp to customers in Western Europe including Germany. Although dilapidated, traces of the production plant still exist today on the outskirts of Plovdiv.

Change in Government

Then abruptly things changed politically. The new government started seizing the land of all its citizens, launching protests among the population. Repression from the government had already started. An organized resistance developed in my dad's town and it was put down. In those days, enrollment in the army was a compulsory requirement of citizenship. One day my father ran into a young man who had deserted the Bulgarian army. Dad was compassionate and kind in spirit so he helped him hide and cared for him as he did his own workers. Unfortunately, the militia found the deserter and chased him into a vineyard where he was subsequently shot and killed. Citizens from the neighboring city were involved and an investigation was launched. Although my dad had nothing to do with the shooting, he was sentenced to 20 years of hard labor for aiding the young man. Evidently this man had been part of the land grab resistance and was heavily involved with the organization against the Communists. Dad was arrested while selling his apple harvest in Plovdiv.

If I said I knew what life was like in Bulgaria in the 1950's when my father reluctantly left Bulgaria, I would be lying. How can a naïve American understand anything about Communism, Socialism or even war at home? I knew very little about the Cold War which would impact my life more than I knew.

For my father's family whose livelihood depended on their ability to grow agriculture, life as they knew it was rapidly changing. In the old world, Socialism had crept in like a thief under the guise of reform for the benefit of all. It demanded the consolidation of family-owned land that had been held for generations into state-run working farms. Without the consent of the citizens, Bulgarians became limited to owning only a quarter of an acre each. My family owned a lot of land, much of it cultivated by hard work and they weren't about to give it away. Dad was interested in *comasatsia* or combining the fields through exchange in order to have a larger parcel that was easier to cultivate but he was not interested in giving it away to the government. If they knew then what would transpire later, their first choice would have been to keep the family together at all costs even if it meant to lose the farm 'but hindsight is 20/20.'

Island of Persin

The 1950's era was a critical point in time with the Bulgarian Communist Party (BCP) according to people who were repressed at the time. A country that once helped them defeat the Turkish rule of over 500 years helped defeat the great resolve of a sovereign nation without some citizens even realizing it. Even today you will find people who are unaware of the system of forced labor camps that existed killing tens of thousands of their own countrymen. Anyone who was deemed an enemy of the state was arrested. Turks, Jews, Christians, farmers, doctors, pastors, and entrepreneurs alike were put on trial, forced to agree to false accusations and sentenced to hard labor or even death. Many were not even afforded trials. Adults and children died as a result.

Bulgaria was not alone in this nightmare in Eastern Europe. Just because they were friends before did not mean that the Soviets had their best interests in mind this time. Bulgarians treated USSR as if they were the big "protective" brother, allowing whatever Stalinist propaganda they chose. Eastern Bloc States like East Germany, Poland, Hungary, Romania, and Czechoslovakia were also victims. It was the Soviet occupation that took Bulgaria down. Many were sent to the Soviet system of forced-labor camps called Gulags. In essence, they were concentration camps.

A forced labor camp with one of the worst reputations was on an island in the Danube River called Persin. This land was once owned by a Bulgarian family when it was an agrarian peasant society. This prison off the north coast of Bulgaria below Romania became known as Belene. Thousands of people including my dad were sent to this dungeon of an island where they were starved, overworked and tortured. A source of food for the region growing vegetables such as leeks due to its sandy wet marshland became a field of death of its own.

On Belene, men were broken of all hopes and dreams of ever escaping. The living conditions were incomprehensible. The goal of Communism was to break all willpower so that a man became hopeless without any individual goals or identity. The men were chased by armed guards with dogs to their daily work detail before dawn. Some men were trampled and left behind in the field to die. No one really knows the number of people who were killed here.

Here dad met a head of military intelligence during World War II named Alexi who had been imprisoned several times. Together they set out to escape the camp. While being forced to dig their own graves moments before their deaths, they found an opportunity to escape. Many had tried but few had survived such a risky maneuver. Maybe it was by chance, a timing thing or the grace of God that the two men did escape and dad lived - with survivor's guilt - to reluctantly tell the story. The job of telling his story has been left to us, his descendants, keeping his memory alive.

Chapter 2. Surviving the Escape

The Dark Blue Danube

On a cloudy evening in the fall of 1953, the water of the river was unusually dark. Once in the river, the men had already tossed their shirts away from them so that the armed guards would target the shirts and not their bodies as they swam away from the guards. The moonless night was cover for them to disappear into the dark. The current of the river was moving the trunk of a tree away from the island so with both hands, dad clutched on to the natural flotation device. It was the only thing keeping him from drowning because he was never much of a swimmer. The river was wide and he needed to cross over to the other side. As he looked behind him, he saw the shadow of the imposing island. He heard the dogs barking and the shrill of the guards' whistles blowing. With every nerve in his body, he could feel the fear of death at the same time sensing the hope of an escape by those left back at the camp. His thoughts went to the other prisoners.

With all the commotion, everyone in the camp knew there was an attempted escape and the guards would be extra-brutal. As if the crushing of the guards' clubs wasn't enough, it was the ones left behind who would pay for the freedom of the two escapees. More work, more beatings and less food were the punishment for an attempted escape but it is what gave those left behind hope. The only prisoners who were able to survive were those who were able to hide this hope in the most intimate place of their hearts. It was a bit of a mind-game.

While in the river the distance between my dad and his friend grew. Alexi didn't need a tree to float him as he was confidently swimming off to the side moving farther and farther away. Then dad lost sight of him. Alexi was much stronger because he was a trained military officer, able to use the strength of his arms to carry him away faster. The frigid water was all around them and the safety of the Romanian shore was still far away. Fighting his own fear, dad hugged the tree trunk with one arm while using the other arm to paddle his way through the night. The cold water was both his friend and enemy. It carried him away from the island and kept him alert, although he had to continually move his limbs to keep from developing hypothermia. He fought the water for hours but he knew that soon the dark river would make room for the morning. He had to be bold yet calm and go with the flow. The water was his salvation as it floated him to the safety of the Romanian shore.

By morning, once ashore, both men reunited and hid in the bushes while drying their remaining clothes in the sun of the day. They rested to regain their strength while continuing to hear the barking of the dogs and the blowing of the whistles. For the next few nights, they stayed close to the shore of the river moving east with the current. As they traveled, they left the noise of the island behind. The families that lived along the river had their own dogs guarding the small family farms. They had to be careful not to alert the farm dogs for fear the barking would expose them. Their senses were so awakened from living on the island prison, that they learned to use their hearing keenly.

Once they were far enough from the island, they chose a location in the river to cross back into Bulgaria at night. This time dad found gourds that he used under his arms to help float him across the river.

"How are your feet?" Alexi asked dad.

Dad ignored him pretending not to hear the question. He didn't want to bring any more attention to the discomfort he felt. Honestly, he just wanted to keep moving. The river water healed the wounded feet but not his heart. The faces of his family members flashed before him. He wondered if he would ever see them again.

The Stars Guided Them

After leaving Romania, they traveled by foot through the Danubian Plain and reached Stara Planina. Every step they took away from the prison took them to a life of freedom. Travelling only at night, the stars guided them. During the day, they foraged for food and rested. They found refuge in the kolibi or farmer's huts made of sticks and straw used for shelter during the rain and very hot summers. At times, they found food, clothing, and survival items here. They continued to move south.

One time, while travelling through the Balkans as they climbed down a steep ravine, they were seen by armed militia who fired shots at them. The trees and shrubs around them took the hits as they evaded capture. They weighed their options. They could continue searching for food in the farming huts all the way to Greece moving further south each night or take the chance of returning home. The journey to Greece would take more than a month and winter was already upon them. They could hide in the mountains near either of the men's villages. They were both aware of the danger to their respective families. The lack of vitamins and salt in their diets was already taking a toll on their health. It took several weeks of trekking through Bulgaria to arrive near Plovdiv.

It happened that on the first frost of the season in 1953, they made it to my family's village on the outskirts of Plovdiv. They selfishly yearned for a full night's rest among their loved ones who could care for them even if it was just for a short time. Neither man had slept for more than a few hours at a time since they escaped. They huddled shoulder-to-shoulder in dad's apple orchard as they considered what to do. If the neighbors saw them enter one of the homesteads, they might report them to the corrupt authorities. They could be set up by Communist sympathizers and have to endure another ambush by militia. If they passed my dad's village and headed for the Rhodope Mountains, they would be trapped for the winter in inhospitable terrain. Unable to start a fire in the woods, they would freeze to death. If they made it to a monastery like Bachkovo in which to take refuge, even that was not safe from the regime. Dad and Alexi's clothes were already thread bare and ragged and they knew they could not physically continue to move further south at this time.

The border with Greece was strictly guarded behind the 'Iron Curtain' and the border guards fired on the spot without warning so the crossing point had to be considered carefully. Once in Greece, they could find a refugee camp and apply for political asylum but that would have to wait several uneasy months.

Chapter 3. Unsafe in the Village

They knew they had to spend the winter somewhere. Dad recognized the hedge row and the mulberry tree line was identifiable even in the dark. The men rested their tired feet under the walnut tree that grew behind the homestead. Dad bent over and kissed the ground beneath it. He got up and walked toward the family's animal stable. His mare named Rosa saw him from a distance and started snorting. Her ears perked up and she started to nervously step with her front hooves. It had been a long time since she had seen him yet she hadn't forgotten. The last time he had seen her, she was pulling the apple cart that he took to Plovdiv to sell the harvest of apples. That was when he was arrested and hadn't been home since. He was so happy to see her. Only this season, the apples hadn't been harvested. They lay rotting on the ground. His family hadn't had enough help to take care of all the field work. He bent over and picked up one of the apples and its aroma filled his senses reminding him of the good times he had with his family on the farm.

Then all of a sudden, he heard the voice of one of his workers, George, who had lived with the family for years. He immediately stooped down to avoid George from seeing him. Although the voice was familiar it seemed deeper than he remembered. George had matured in the time he'd been imprisoned. He was loading the hay in the cart for the animals. The idea of sneaking into the cart and hiding under the hay came to mind. Once inside the property, it would be difficult to get back out. The militia were on duty taking turns surveilling his property all day long. This time there were no ravines to escape down like in the Balkans or bushes to hide in along a river, so they had to move quickly without being seen.

The grim realization of placing the whole family in danger became a reality. If they were caught anywhere near the property, it would be bad news. No matter which decision they made, the sentence for the two men was the same. Could he live with himself if anyone else was killed? They could either die from a gunshot wound or die in the mountains. They were already sentenced to death for escaping Belene. The truth was no one was safe. The family was already in danger because of the stranglehold the entire country was under. Anyone could be unjustly arrested and sent to one of the labor camps or killed. No crime had to be committed. He quickly ran back to Alexi and told him to get up because they were going to sneak into the homestead by hiding in the hay cart.

The daily fieldwork drained George of his strength and he couldn't wait to get back to his new wife in the village. He walked toward Rosa and rebuked her for her odd behavior as he untied her. It was late and he still had to make it over to the nearby river because the animal needed water and as usual, she waited patiently for him to finish his work. He could not figure out why she was acting so strangely tonight. Maybe she was nervous because she saw another animal nearby. George patted her on the back to try to calm her and took her for the water. Dad and Alexi took the opportunity to quickly make room in the back of the cart and buried themselves beneath the hay. They heard the footsteps of George and Rosa as they made their way back to the cart. The cart jerked and took off making a screeching sound from the additional weight of the two men. The mare continued to act nervously. Her ears twitched, nose snorted and she was very alert. George kept coaxing and speaking to her. As he walked alongside Rosa, he calmed her. They moved closer to the village and the house windows were already dark and the streets were empty. There was a dead-end street called a *chakmak sokak* behind their parcel of land. Near it was the gate through which they had to pass. It was designed in such a way that after passing through it, the path led straight into the barn. Near the gate in the dark stood one of the militiamen. The mare walked slowly but steadily for she knew her way to the barn even in the darkness. Someone coughed loudly and Rosa slowed down. George jumped out of the cart, taking the harness and walked next to the mare.

"Stop! It's a checkpoint," spoke the loud mean voice.

"Good evening," said George.

"I'm coming home for the night with the hay."

"Oh, it's you, *ahmak* (stupid idiot) said the same loud voice.

"Are you still working for these *kulatzi?*" (rich people opposed to the new orders).

With his head down in dread, George's spirit sank. Besides, he had no idea he was carrying the two fugitives in the hay cart and now even his life was in danger.

This guard was one of the worst bullies in the village and was disliked for his brutality especially by dad's wife who was beaten by him after dad was arrested. Now he hung out as part of the government enforcements surveilling the entire property on the lookout for dad. George was accustomed to his condescending remarks and arrogance. He ignored him and silently continued to walk to the gate. He opened the gate carefully guiding the cart inside. Rosa stopped under the awning near the farmhouse where the hay and grains were stored. He started to unhitch Rosa and planned on attending to the hay in the morning.

While still under the hay, dad and Alexi heard another set of footsteps. This time it was Grandfather Kiro. He was the only one still awake in the house and had been waiting for the worker to return from the field. He asked George,

"Kid, why you so late? I will untie Rosa and feed her. Get home to your wife!"

Dad realized that George was married. The last letter he had received while at Belene spoke of George's engagement. He wondered if George and his new bride lived on the land that he had picked out for George years ago. He longed to talk to the young man like they did before.

Grandpa had already prepared food for Rosa and noticed she was acting nervously.

"Is he still outside?" He asked George in a whispered voice as he nodded his head towards the gate. George nodded yes.

"You get home! God will punish the evil man out there in His own time."

The guards came every day but Grandpa Kiro didn't know if his son was dead or alive. No one had heard from dad and he longed to know the truth. Looking up to the heavens, he whispered under his breath.

"Remember us oh Lord, help us get through this hardship." After unhitching Rosa, freeing her from the harness, he fed her and wiped the sweat off her sleek body. She continued lifting her head, looking behind and making noises. Grandpa figured she just didn't like the man outside the gate and he didn't blame her. As he was comforting her, he spoke to her as if he was comforting his own soul with his words.

"Rosa, tomorrow you will need to work again, but for now eat and rest." He walked her to the stable he had cleaned and she began eating.

Grandpa Kiro's Burdened Heart

That night, like many other nights, Grandpa Kiro's heart was burdened for his family. Just a few days earlier, the school teacher brought the entire class of students to the front entrance of his home. As the children were lined up, at the teacher's command, they shouted in unison,

"Here lives an enemy of the state!" His own grandson, Vasil, was at the back of the line pale and barely mouthing the words he was told to repeat. They were brought there to make fun of him. He felt intimidated and bent over in shame because they were rallying against his own family. Upon hearing the noise, Grandma Luba marched over to the boy and took him out of line. He didn't dare look into the eyes of his classmates or his grandmother.

"It's a shame you now use the children to do your dirty work!" cried grandmother.

She wondered how this child could live with this label among his peers. Did he understand what was happening with the family? The Communists used many people including neighbors to accomplish their work as spies. Vasil's friend, Dinko, didn't even seem right. He followed Vasil into the stable and the apple orchard as if he was looking for something. Even in the house he was always listening to the conversations of the adults. Such was life in the oppressive home of an 'Enemy of the State.' Spy or not, the child needed a friend. Dinko, as unclean as he was, sufficed.

After tending to Rosa, Grandpa Kiro headed back to the house to go to bed. The gas light in the window of the house went out. Dad and Alexi were afraid to move out of the cart. Only a stone fence separated them from the guard with the rifle outside. They were cold and stiff under the hay and had to move their limbs. They could hear the steps of the militia as they made their rounds causing their hearts to beat faster. Making a hole in the hay to see out the cart, they found an opportune time to make their way quietly to the stable where the animals were kept.

Once inside the barn, the reality hit that the whole family could be executed for their sake. Besides, dad felt a responsibility to his friend, Alexi. Together they survived the escape, the rough Bulgarian terrain and the dangers on the road. He owed his life to him and he also needed protection. It would be best for the two men to split up at this time to be cared for by trusted family members. Safely in the barn, they needed to rest and could think about this tomorrow. Being home, as dangerous as it was, felt good as they fell asleep huddling in the piles of grain warming each other back-to-back.

After about an hour, dad woke up and climbed towards the beams of the roof lifting a tile to make a lookout. Even as tired as he was, he couldn't get back to sleep. He wanted to see the location of the guards. From here he could learn their habits and find out when their shifts changed. At a little before dawn, everything was quiet and still. He could not see the guards. On the other side of the barn he did the same thing. Removing a clay tile from the roof, he could see the house and the path to the barn from this angle. He knew that Grandfather Kiro would be the first in the barn that morning to care for the animals.

Dad came down from the roof to where Rosa was standing. He smiled when he sensed she remembered him. He brought a little hay, petted her and laid down the food he prepared for the oxen. As he went about cleaning the stable, replacing the old hay with the new, he felt at home and forgot his cares.

Then he heard his father coughing as he headed up the path to the barn. Dad was startled back to reality and hid behind the barn door. Grandpa Kiro opened the door to find that the animals were already eating and the hay had been replaced. He stood puzzled wondering who may have been there because he was usually the first to arrive. It was too early for the workers to be there.

"Dad, it's me," said father to Grandpa Kiro.

"What are you doing here, son? There are evil people looking for you."

"Don't worry dad, we outsmarted them and hid in the hay last night. We even made it past the guard!"
Tears were falling down their faces. His outstretched arms welcomed his son home.

"Wait, let me take a look at you. You've lost a lot of weight and your clothes are torn, dear child. God help us!"

"Dad, be quiet don't cry, there's another man with me, Alexi. I am going to take him to Aunt Vessela's home. She won't be able to turn him away; she has a big heart. Both of us cannot stay here."

"Son, we cannot trouble one more house. The times are very difficult and there are guards everywhere. They are like blood-thirsty hounds and no one can be trusted these days."

"We need to spend the winter somewhere until the weather passes. We will see what to do after winter. Tell me how everyone is. How's my wife? How are the kids and mom?"

"They are okay, son. Your mom cries quietly after everyone goes to sleep. Your wife is strong. The older girls have matured and the younger kids are at ease. Vasil leaves the house and is gone all day on the horse. He is so free-spirited and wild but his heart is good. There is so much to talk about. I am sure you are cold and hungry. Let me bring you food and clothes."

"Only tell mom. Don't tell anyone else," dad said.

"Okay son, okay. I will be back shortly," replied Grandpa as he looked troubled. The old man looked smaller and bent over. As he started toward the house, dad noticed how grandpa's hair had greyed since he had seen him. The harsh conditions they were living under had taken a toll on them all.

The Winter of 1953

Dad's wife, Ruska, along with my grandparents, Kiro and Luba, continued to take care of him through the winter of 1953-54. He lived in the barn with the horses hiding from the militia. Alexi, lived with my Aunt Vessela, hidden away somewhere in the village. The older girls, Anelia and Tanya, were already married by this time. My youngest sister, Blagorodna, often played in the yard during the sunny winter days. Dad could only watch her from a distance before someone would nervously scold her to come inside so she wouldn't stumble upon him in the stable. They also had to keep Dinko, the nosey neighbor, out of the barn. Occasionally dad was able to watch his granddaughter, Boyana, play with a ball outside the barn door. He enjoyed these times because he was able to see his children and granddaughter from a distance.

My brother, Vasil, a bit bullheaded and unruly, helped Grandpa Kiro feed the livestock in the barn. Initially, the boy did not know dad was in the barn as he hid from him. Of the four children, dad saw Vasil the most because he spent a lot of time with Rosa. Dad hid above in a rafter. He observed how his son had grown and watched as he took extra care of Rosa giving her lots of attention. He gave the best grain and the softest hay to the highly favored mare and in return she took him wherever he wanted to go. He hurried to make food for the oxen and laid the hay out for them to sleep on but he'd always go to Rosa who he loved the most. When he saddled her to take her out through the small door to the back street away from Grandma Luba's view, the mare carried the two of them out to the large field behind the property. Once out in the field, dad would go to the highest beam and again remove a roof tile to watch Rosa gallop away with his son until the boy and the mare were a mere dot on the white snowy field. Dad spent hours up on that roof in anticipation of his son's return home. The coldness of the winter and the folly of the boy worried him.

While up on the roof, he looked for the round red glow of the cigarette of the armed guards in the darkness. As usual, they were there taking turns every hour surveilling his property. He still marveled at how he was able to sneak past them while in the hay cart that memorable fall night but he had no idea how he was going to get back out safely.

Eventually Vasil would stumble upon father in the barn that winter. Only the two of them and God knows how this reunion went. My brother remained in Bulgaria for the remainder of his life.

Chapter 4. Seasons Come and Seasons Go

The Spring of 1954

Come spring, the police notified our family that the fugitives were dead. They doubted the men survived the harsh winter or frigid river. If this was to further intimidate my relatives or test their reaction to the news, it was not known. These were their tactics. If they were found, the men would be executed on the spot. It must have been difficult for Kiro and Luba to hide their emotions. They and Ruska knew the truth and they guarded the secret with their lives.

During the last month in hiding as times became more dangerous, only Grandma Luba was willing to take the chance of delivering food to dad. In the Spring of 1954 on the second Sunday before Lent, it was decided that the two political prisoners would once again take a chance to escape Bulgaria. For them, the arrival of spring meant it was time to depart the family's village. They left without being able to say good-bye. They returned to the road heading south to Greece. They hoped to save the two households from further risk. Their plan was to stay in Greece until the political climate changed and it was safe to return home or try to gain political asylum elsewhere. My family lost track of our father for an unknown length of time. It was too dangerous for them to know anything. This kept the family safe but detrimentally impacted my 14-year-old brother for life; wishing he could have gone with him.

Travelling through Bulgaria again only at night, they made it to the border falling into a refugee camp and claimed political asylum in Greece. Although dad and Alexi arrived together, a vehicle showed up and ushered Alexi away. The Greek authorities provided no further explanation. To them, Alexi was an educated man able to speak several languages and proved to be more valuable than my dad, the farmer. Alexi exchanged information and worked for the US Army Intelligence in Greece, and was quickly transferred to the

United States of America. This separated the two friends by class and distance. It was rumored that he became a spy for the Americans.

The Summer of 1954

The waves crashed against the rocky seashore; rolling back and forth into the Mediterranean Sea. The sound of screeching sea gulls and the salty air reminded dad that he was no longer in Bulgaria. The sun setting behind him made his shadow look like a large ghost in front of him. The shadow, like his future, loomed ahead like an unknown dark force. He could hear unintelligible voices coming from a nearby Greek village. It was just another day like the one before. Nothing ever changed at the migrant camp except the tides. Although relatively safe, it was excruciating to be there. Time stood still. Dad always hoped in anticipation that something would change with his status. All he could do was wait until he was moved by the authorities to another location.

He remembered the night of the escape and thought the most difficult time of his life was over but this waiting was the hardest part. From the window of his room as he sat alone, he looked over the waves and wondered what lie ahead. He had no news from his friend and it gnawed at him. At the same time, it was impossible to contact his family because if the authorities intercepted any communication, the family would again be at risk. Not knowing when he could move out of the camp, it became a prison of its own.

Greece in 1956

Greece is no stranger to immigrants. Today the immigrants flocking there are from places like Syria. They are on the same path looking for freedom more than a half century later. When my father was there in the 1950's, it was to escape the clutches of the Bulgarian Communist Party (BCP). After living in a migrant camp for two years, he was admitted to a mechanical training school. There he made a new friend 27 years younger by the name of Ivan who would become a lifelong friend.

Although the training school was not a labor camp, it was still a dangerous place. As told to me by "Uncle" Ivan, it happened that one Sunday morning between 7 and 8 A.M., two men in suits arrived at the door of the school. The men told a fellow student that they were there to give dad and Ivan important papers for them to return to Bulgaria. They pretended as if they were trying to help. While shaking one of the men's hands, dad glanced out a window and noticed a black KGB-style car parked under a mulberry tree. The engine was still running and the back door was ajar. Immediately, he thought it was suspicious. He instinctively reached over and grabbed a broom from a utility closet swinging it horizontally. With both hands on the broom, he pushed the men out the door. After they were over the threshold, he quickly locked it.

A few weeks prior to this incident, two other Bulgarian men had been pushed out the eighth-floor windows to their deaths for an unknown reason. Not knowing who the real target was, my father reported the new incident to the police in Athens which helped to expedite their Green Cards. It seemed that danger followed him but the hand of God was always upon him.

PART II

LIFE AS AN AMERICAN

Chapter 5. The Immigrant

Father came to the United States of America as a legal immigrant. The hardships he experienced did not give him the right to enter the country illegally. He needed a sponsor. He prayed for a sponsor. Dad didn't find his sponsor, his sponsor found him. Bogdan Vazov took personal and financial responsibility for dad and invited him to Buffalo, New York helping him settle in the new land. Actually, dad and Ivan were unknowingly sponsored by the same man, one week apart. Both arrived in Western New York and met, with great joy, at a community meeting. Far from their loved ones and way of life, they became each other's family. The Buffalo-Bulgarian community grew one man at a time.

One Man Sponsors 27 Immigrants

I know little about Bogdan, the kind-hearted and generous sponsor, except that he was a chemical engineer. Everything I learned about Bogdan was from Ivan and my niece, Rositsa. As the men arrived here, he took it upon himself to financially support them, providing a home for 15 days each; helping them on their feet. It was a great opportunity for the men to live and work in the United States of America. The men usually arrived by plane in pairs but my dad may have flown alone. Ivan and my father were two of 27 men who were taken under the wing of Mr. Vazov. He assisted dad in gaining employment. Not only did he help them look for jobs, he always tried to keep track of them after they settled in the city.

Bogdan had already left Bulgaria 20 years earlier. He was tireless in his sponsorship for one very poignant reason. He always hoped that one of the recipients would be one of his own family members left behind. Bogdan was looking for his younger brother who, much like my father, had been spirited away due to alleged crimes against the Communist regime. I never learned his brother's name but he had a sister named Gabby. Gabby's son was a lecturer at the Mining and Geology University in Bulgaria. Sadly, Bogdan's family member never crossed the ocean. Bogdan's siblings weren't the only ones left behind in the old country. So were mine. By continuing to sponsor others, Bogdan's loss became our gain. How can we, as the descendants of Bogdan's 27 men, ever thank him enough for giving the foreigners the chance for a life of freedom?

Alexi was my dad's age and his sons, Mitko and Stoyan, were around the same age as my brother. I never learned the details of Alexi's immigration process. He was not one of Bogdan's 27 men because he was brought over as an aid to the government of the USA. He left Greece a few years before dad and lived in Washington, D.C.

While my niece, Rositsa, was in college her dad visited the shore of Belene to see the island and the river's tumultuous past. There he wept for dad and his loneliness. My brother waited years for the chance to live in the United States of America with dad but his dream never came true. He died in 1997 at the age of 59 while watching his own grandchildren grow up in the old country.

Alexi's mother named Helga often came to visit my family in the small village. She and my Grandmother Luba would shut themselves in a room away from the children and talk about something secret; the whereabouts of their sons. Alexi's wife, Lila, also visited my Bulgarian family but eventually she immigrated to the United States of America with their two boys. Sadly, Lila died in 1965. Their sons, went on to graduate from college and became successful professionals.

Starting Over

Dad started out in the new world as a dish washer but this was not his strength. After spending so many years as part of an affluent Bulgarian society, it was a difficult adjustment. He was accustomed to running a large business with Grandpa Kiro and dreaming of expanding their strawberry fields and apple orchards. He was thankful to be alive and safe but many times he worried about how his family was surviving without him. His parents were already aged. His only son was a young teen when he left. Thankfully, two of his daughters found loving husbands. Still, Ruska bore the brunt of the burden raising the younger children without her husband. She never remarried.

Not knowing the English language and leaving the only family he knew behind was lonely. At this point dad was already middle aged. Bogdan was able to help him find a better job as the janitor of a Buffalo city high school, not a glamorous job, but a job that he did well to support himself and eventually his new family. His real passion, however, was horticulture and it harkened to his life in Bulgaria. Both Buffalo and Southern Bulgaria have similar climates and being the innovative agricultural man from the old country he went to work on the farm. This is what he knew best. Running two greenhouses and a flower shop well into his 60's may have served as some small comfort to the man who was forced to leave everything and everyone behind.

My dad was 46 years old when he arrived in the United States of America. Eleven years later, I was born. In the late 1960's, his Bulgarian family became his past. He fell in love with my mom, a beautiful young lady, and soon after, I was born. The 57-year old sang Bulgarian songs, taught me Bulgarian dances and how to appreciate nature and animals.

My mother was young and soon after she realized her life with this old man was not what she really wanted. She fell in love with a younger man who was more suited for her. I went with my mom and left my dad behind. All attempts by my father to see me were in vain.

Chapter 6. City Living

B efore I was born, during the 1960's, my father purchased his apartment building at 988 Genesee Street as a property tax foreclosure from the City of Buffalo. I remember the address so vividly because the numbers 9-8-8 were arranged in black and white penny-sized tiles on the storefront entrance. Many times, my feet crossed over these numbers as I played with friends running in and out of the flower shop without a care in the world. As with many buildings in this part of town, it was in rough shape but this did not deter my father from working on the building to make it habitable for all of us. These buildings were wood structures and over time, many of them became condemned and demolished. Buffalo hit its prime at the turn of the 20th century but by the 1970's, the population had started moving to the suburbs leaving the city behind.

There was an empty lot next door with many weeds growing in place of the structure that had been there. According to my aunt, the old structure had burned and killed the children inside. This is the same aunt who would later help me find my father. One winter I remember receiving ice skates for Christmas and I found a patch of ice on this vacant lot in which to ice skate. One summer, armed with a weed whacker, I cut the weeds down until I got a sliver from a prickly bush in my eye. That put an end to playing in the vacant lot. I remember dad coming home late from the countryside greenhouse the day this occurred. He consoled me as I laid flat on the living room sofa with a cold cloth on my sore eye provided by mom.

Across the street was the neighborhood funeral parlor where my cat would roam when she escaped. On the other side of the vacant lot going east was a local store selling cigarettes and convenience items. My dad bought his Lucky Strike cigarettes from this store from time to time as he parked his station wagon along the side of the building. Next door going west towards downtown was the neighborhood pub where my mom tended bar, cooked and waitressed. I practically lived in this pub; always stopping at lunch time during the school year to eat a bowl of chili and oyster crackers before returning to my Catholic school a short distance away. The owners of the bar were more affluent and lived in the suburbs. They became good friends of ours, treating me like a princess and always appreciating my mom's hard work.

One year as I was in the restaurant's pantry replenishing the cracker bin for my mom, I looked on the top shelf and all my Christmas presents were already purchased and hidden away. I never admitted that I saw the gifts as I was in awe of how many there were. That year I received a big dollhouse to go with the large doll mom and dad gave me. I remember pretending to talk on the phone in the pub's phone booth with its narrow accordion style door. My mom and I spent time together in the large commercial kitchen and I played with the owner's German Shepherd who guarded the place at night. Was it the best place for a child to spend time? Perhaps not but I have more good memories of this neighborhood bar than bad. The people that I met loved me and treated me well even if they were drinking. My dad never drank and he disliked that my mom worked there. He always asked her to quit that job. She did, eventually, but only after it was too late.

Our home was in a three-story apartment building with a storefront on the ground level, two apartments on the second floor and a very roomy flat on the third floor complete with a built-in bird cage in the kitchen. It even had a dishwasher - no small luxury in those days. The small back yard had no grass as it was completely paved with concrete and included a steep steel children's slide. My friends who lived in the apartment across the hall taught me how to run up the slide from the bottom. This proved to be a bad idea after falling down the slide hitting the pavement again injuring my eye. Dad was not happy about this. Eventually this slide would be removed and the entire back yard became a glass greenhouse with rows of raised beds constructed of wood full of growing plants. Overhead were pipes soldiered together into an irrigation system most likely similar to that in the old country.

It was in the third-floor apartment that Alexi lived with us for a while. My mom remembers that while he was with us, he was a broadcaster with the radio program "Voice of America." He would have been very well-known to the Buffalo-Bulgarian community.

My mom came from a very large family. My grandparents, aunts and uncles (some of them already married at this point) rented dad's apartments. This was how my parents met. By the time I was born, none of the extended family remained in the building. Originally, we lived on the upper floor but for whatever reason dad moved us to the second floor when I was two or three. The upper floor apartment was drafty and we had plastic on some of the windows to insulate against the cold winters of Buffalo. One of my mom's younger brothers was interested in moving into the third floor flat but shortly after I moved out, this uncle was killed at the age of 23 by a gang. No one else ever lived in the third-floor apartment after that.

I remember the smaller apartment on the second floor where I spent the most time was cozy with a wood-burning stove. It was this stove's pipe on which my mom injured her back when she was six months pregnant that forced her into labor prematurely. She had been helping dad install a new linoleum floor in the apartment. Being so premature, I was never expected to survive weighing only two pounds. They thought I was a miracle and I'm sure they were happy albeit a bit nervous to bring me home from the hospital. Everyone doted on me and my grandmother said they could carry me in a shoebox because I was so tiny. Just like my dad's tiny plant seedlings, I grew and thrived.

In this second-floor apartment I learned to read. I baked cakes for dad with my Easy Bake Oven while reading my books to him. He couldn't read English. This apartment had a large coat closet in the living room near the entrance. This is where they stored my toys. One day, when I was looking for something, I found my cat who had been missing for days. She was in the closet with a litter of kittens. The kittens were better than any toy I could find. As I pulled a kitten out to show my mom, she screamed thinking it was a mouse and I was startled and dropped the poor kitten to the kitchen floor. Thankfully the momma cat accepted the kitten as I returned it to the closet.

We had fish, frogs, cats and birds in the middle of the city. My dad also loved dogs and had a beautiful Alaskan husky. Upon the few times I visited him after we moved out, I saw that he had tamed a wild bird and kept it with him in our old apartment. He clearly had a way with animals and loved them all. If anyone was one with nature, it was him.

I spent seven years in this home with both parents. I only remember about five of these years. Supposedly, the first memory we can recall says something about us. I wish I knew more about my dad which is one of the reasons I searched for my family for so long. They had answers I needed.

Fishing on the Niagara River

My earliest remembrance of life was aboard a small fishing boat on the great Niagara River which borders New York State and Canada. The boat was full with my mom's family. I was about two or three years of age, of course, too young to truly remember details. My mom's youngest sister who is five years older than me remembers that day on the river clearly. According to her, dad saved her life. I don't recall the specific memory myself, but he caught her from falling overboard. I am not sure we were wearing life jackets. Maybe the children were and the adults were not. I can only imagine because even seatbelts were barely mandatory in the 1970's.

As we cruised the waterway on the motorized boat, what I recall was that everyone except dad and I were afraid of the water. I remember that dad was asking the family if they wanted to go left or right of the land that jutted out of the river ahead. The consensus was that they didn't want to go in either direction. They were fearful of the engine failing and the boat drifting over the falls. Their decision forced us to return to the dock. I remember the family being relieved to be back on solid ground and it was apparent that the adults in the boat thought he was being reckless.

After thinking about this memory, I realized that in life we are sometimes faced with decisions when we are at a crossroads. At the fork in the road or river in this case, we had the choice to go left or right. Instead, we turned around and went back to the starting point. Sometimes we miss out on a journey we could have had.

Dad fished there many times before, which may have been the reason why he knew the river so well. He was not afraid of drifting over the falls. There must be a reason why this memory was my first but I've not figured it out. I may not actually remember fishing there myself but after being raised in Western New York, this river has always been a favorite place to visit. In my mind, Niagara Falls and the image of my dad go hand-in-hand. A decade earlier, in a very different part of the world, he swam another tumultuous river escaping with his life. His escape across the Danube River was a story he rarely told and preferred to forget. The first I heard of the story was after my son was born in the late 1990's.

Although my dad was always busy with the repairs on the building, his greenhouse in the countryside, and his job as a janitor at the school, he found time to fish. One morning on a school day, he left with his fishing boat for the river where he found solace. When I came home from school, my mom and dad were in the only bathroom discussing something unusual. When I went to see what the commotion was all about, I found them peering over the side of the cast-iron claw-foot bathtub filled to the brim with fish dad had caught on that fishing trip. They were all alive and swimming around the oval white porcelain enclosure. My mother was aghast. "Where are we going to bathe?" she asked.

"At the sink" dad replied which was about three feet away. This was no place for a little girl to bathe she insisted pointing at me and under no circumstances was she going to allow this.

"You have one day to get these fish out of here" she scolded while pointing at me.

"By the time she gets home from school tomorrow, they had better be gone!"

It may have been his intention to keep the fish alive by feeding them. He saw nothing wrong with this concept of keeping them as pets and cooking them as needed. He was trying to be a good provider and enable us to eat the freshest fish possible. This may have been fine for a country dweller, but not for us city folk. There was a time in his life when a fish the size of these would feed many men. I remember returning home the next day after school and as I ran to the bathtub still in my school uniform to check on the fish, the bathtub was empty. Most likely, he transported them back to the river in five-gallon buckets where he was the day before and released them. I was so sad to see them gone. I don't remember eating any fish for dinner.

Chapter 7. The Greenhouse Business

The scents that I remember most from the greenhouse aside from the pungent odor of the fertilizer were the coffee brewing in the electric pot, fresh tomatoes on the vine and green peppers frying in the electric skillet. One weekend in the summer during the height of the vegetable season, we worked later than normal. My dad always worked late but for some reason I remember this day with my mom and grandmother because I got sick. They often worked with him tending the plants and selling fruits and vegetables at the side of the road. We had everything… corn, tomatoes, peppers, onions, eggplant, strawberries, even flowers too.

We had an abundance of sweet bell peppers this day. Being so busy, we missed our normal dinner time and as my mom and dad discussed what to make, my grandmother suggested we slice up several green peppers and sauté them. The smell of these home-grown peppers was incredible. That's all we ate for dinner that night, forkfuls of tender green peppers. I can still taste the sweetness of them like candy. I long for the heirloom peppers that taste just as good as they smell. Even today as I cook them, I am reminded of this simple way to eat them.

In addition to the smell of the peppers, dad brewed a pot of rich coffee. He drank it with both milk and sugar. It smelled so good that I asked for a drink of it. He saw no reason to deny me. After all, I was about four and getting so big already. He obliged and I drank the whole cup. Nothing I had up to this point tasted as good as this coffee.

After cleaning up, we were happy and full and drove the twenty-mile trip home to our apartment in the city. Not far into our journey, my head was out the window vomiting the night's dinner. My mother insisted it was the coffee. My dad insisted it was the green peppers. My mom told dad never to let me have coffee again. I still love a good cup of coffee exactly the way dad served it that summer night.

The Country Greenhouse

We sold our goods at the side of the road all summer long and into the fall. My mom and her sisters would bring their bicycles and cycle up the big hill in town. Some relatives would come for the day to picnic on the grounds. Others would just visit to marvel at the sights and smells. I am sure none of them went home empty-handed. This greenhouse was a playground for me as it was built next to a large church where I would balance myself by walking on its stone fence before being scolded by the nuns.

As in the old country, my dad was always lending a hand to someone in need. He was handy at repairs and one evening in late fall or early winter, dad had to fix the plumbing in the home of the owners of the country greenhouse. This place also sat on the property near the corner of Main and Davison Streets in the Town of Clarence, New York. My father leased this greenhouse for years. When the owner came to ask assistance in unfreezing his pipes, dad placed me in the car which was in the driveway and told me to stay until he came back. It seemed like eternity that he was gone but the teenagers who lived in another house on the property led me inside the home where dad was working. He emerged full of cobwebs from the crawlspace under the house. He assured me that he would not leave without me. He also had to unfreeze our own pipes at home at the apartment building so he had prior experience with it.

This landowner also sold goods at the side of the road. He was a master leather craftsman. I watched in awe as he used his metal tools pressing fancy designs into leather handbags. One day, he lost one of his favorite tools and asked my dad if I had it because he remembered me looking at it. My mom asked me if I had taken it and when I said "No," dad emphatically told him I did not have it. Then one day as dad was cutting the grass with the lawnmower, he found the tool on the ground where it must have fallen and I think it got bent by the blades of the gas-powered lawnmower. I never saw the landowner again.

The last time I set foot in the country greenhouse was one summer after the break-up when my mom took me to see my dad and he wanted to keep me there with him to enjoy the summer vacation. Because it had no indoor plumbing and I would need to use a camping style toilet and wash in a bucket my mom said "No way!" He didn't mind living this way for he enjoyed the greenhouse in the country and by this time he was all alone.

The City Greenhouse

He also transported his goods to the city where he sold them in our storefront which was his flower shop. Many times, he delivered flower arrangements for customers of the funeral parlors nearby. He gave away flower pens as advertisement. The sides of the stick pens were printed with the name of his business, 'The Price is Right Flower Shop.' That was until the game show contacted him to say he couldn't use their name any more. He didn't care, he continued his business. He would show me the display of artificial flower pens meant for his customers. Each flower was stuck into a large foam heart as he asked me what flower I wanted to write with that day. One day I chose a red rose, other days a yellow sunflower or an orange poppy. Thanks to dad, I had a bouquet full of pens.

Dad loved to grow and sell geraniums, roses, gladiolas and sunflowers. He taught me how to tenderly take the seedlings and gently tap them out of the baby pots to transplant them into their adult pots so we could grow and sell them as big plants. We would gingerly place the main stem of the plant between our index and middle finger as we flipped the pot upside down tapping it with our thumb so that it would fall out of the pot without injuring the roots. He used a lot of terra cotta pots. One weekend, we drove a few hours to visit a clay pot manufacturer. My mom was fearful as we drove our station wagon over the long driveway which contained a layer of clay pot fragments.

"What if we get a flat tire?" She asked. We were so far from home. The greenhouse and flower shop businesses were our life.

The part of town where we lived was not safe from crime even in the 1970's. The East side of the city developed a bad reputation which has continued to this day. One night, our neighbors were babysitting me in their apartment on the second floor. Right below us in the storefront, with plants growing in the back part of the house, dad was mugged. Earlier that day a man had come in pretending to be a customer, even asking for a tour of the back room so he could "case the place." He returned later after dark with a heavy metal pipe for a weapon and struck dad in the head requiring a trip to the emergency room for several stitches. Our neighbor who lived above the pub heard my dad's cry for help and came to his aid. He was relieved that I wasn't in the store with him that night and I was glad he survived. We celebrated the next day as we were back in the country at the greenhouse by eating at the Chinese restaurant down on Main Street. I remember my mom was embarrassed because of the prominent stitches on the side of his head. Maybe he should have worn a hat. This was around the time I was in first grade and attended Bingo with my mom when she volunteered at the Catholic school. After this incident, I remember dad carrying a metal pipe in his left hand under his trench coat whenever he walked me home after dark.

One day while playing in the city with two friends from the neighborhood, we strolled through the ground floor of the flower shop heading out the side door to the empty lot. As we joyfully romped through the place, we found a piece of insulation resembling balled up cotton burning in the middle of the room. We all screamed and jumped over the fire forcing dad to run in from the backyard to see what was the matter. Stomping the fire out with his large shoes, he ushered us outside. Later that evening, we were all questioned by the adults separately who saw the severity of the situation. They wanted to be sure we were not playing with matches. We were good kids. It was the neighborhood that was rough.

My dad designed the greenhouse in the city himself, employing a friend of the family to help install the large plates of glass over metal frames. This was when he removed the children's slide. He was annoyed when neighborhood troubled kids would throw rocks to break the glass for fun causing him to replace the panes constantly. He went so far as to install chicken wire on top of the glass.

"What good will that do?" mom asked inquisitively. He explained that it would catch the large rocks that broke the panes while letting smaller stones through that were too little to cause much damage while still allowing the sunshine in. He was always trying to build something. This allowed him to move away from the greenhouse in the country and grow the plants in the comfort of his own property. He spent less time driving and less money on gas while building his business close to home. It was here that I remember the irrigation system he had built with pipes throughout the greenhouse possibly similar to what he built in the old country.

Leaving it all Behind

One day in second grade it was time to leave. I left my school and the place I called home without anyone knowing except my mom and her family. Dad came home to an empty apartment. I lived with grandma for the following six months and this was when I experienced the air raid drills under my school desk at Buffalo Public School No. 2. My father called my grandmother on the phone asking if he could talk to me but he was not allowed. Eventually I moved with my mom and her new husband to a new place and life changed. I even had a new baby brother. I saw dad only a handful of times from age seven to eleven.

One time we visited him at the apartment building where he had moved from our second-floor apartment down to the first floor. Mom told me his wild bird escaped. Maybe our old apartment was too lonely for him. Or perhaps the apartment was falling apart, because I remember a hole in the bedroom wall the size of a fingertip through which I could see daylight. He had moved his living quarters into a small room off the flower shop. There we sat as he gave me two Christmas presents that were wrapped and waiting for me. Inside the boxes were two pink bathrobes. One robe was for summer and the other was for winter.

The summer robe was a rose-colored thin cotton flannel while the other a lighter blush pink that was quilted. My mom mentioned that they were too small but he explained that he didn't know when he was going to see me. By then, it was no longer Christmas and I had already grown so much. It was too late to return them to the department store so they let me take them home anyway. I wore them into my teenage years until I could no longer pull the sleeves onto my arms. They were the last gifts from him and my last visit to 9-8-8 Genesee Street.

He did this for a few years but by the time he finally moved away from the country location, my mom and I had already left.

Eventually, he left the city greenhouse and moved to the West side of town to Grant Street doing what he knew best, selling plants and flowers including geraniums in a small storefront which reminded him of his old country.

At the Door

I remember the last day I spent with my father as a sixth grader. There was no snow on the ground and I sense it may have been in the fall of the year. When my mom and I arrived at his flower shop on Grant Street, there were men in his shop; two or three Hispanics. He spoke to them and after sending them away, they turned and left. I never found out who the men were except my mom later said they were relatives of his new girlfriend. She gave birth to a girl about eight years younger than me. Although probably living in my own city, I still have not found her; dad's sixth child.

By this time both my mom and dad had moved on. There was a purpose for our visit and it wasn't necessarily a social visit. He was surprised to see us and spoke gently, asking my mom how I was doing. He looked at my teeth and asked my mom to keep an eye on them for cavities. He said that he was worried by the way the adult teeth were growing. I was at that awkward age where my teeth were too large for my face. He had not seen me in a while, possibly a year or two.

After my mom indicated why we were there, he ushered us to the back of the shop where he lived. There he had a twin-sized bed and a 13-inch black and white television. They were probably the same ones I used when I lived with him years earlier in our flat where I watched *Sesame Street* and *The Electric Company* every day while mom worked next door. He offered us something to eat to which we replied, "No, thank you." His half-eaten meal was sitting on a side table, a sign of his unannounced visitors. I'm sure we had already eaten because it was after dinner time. He relaxed a bit when we sat at the edge of his bed, and my mother continued to speak. He seemed agitated but did not let the reason for our visit wreck our time together. He enjoyed our visit and wanted us to stay longer. We were in a hurry and I don't think we stayed longer than an hour.

That night, mom presented dad with prepared adoption papers. She and my step-dad were kindly asking him to voluntarily sign the legal forms to give them legal custody of me to which he again resisted. As we left his shop it felt cold and dark outside, it was almost dusk. We stood outside facing dad as he stood in the doorway.

"Natalie, don't let her forget me" plead dad. None of us had a dry eye. My step-father was home waiting for us. I had a new dad now. This was my last visit to his shop on Grant Street. It was while living here that he decided to return to his Bulgarian family and the land of his birth.

As an adult, I read the court papers which stated "father abandoned child" and my heart sank. I asked myself, how did the court get this so wrong? It would not be the first court motion filed against dad although this one was in English. He had his own trial in his own country of birth which left him without certain rights. As in Bulgaria with four children and in the United States of America with me, abandonment was never his intention. He lost not only one family but at least two. As he eluded to me in his letter many years later dated December 26, 1988:

"...he thinks of you just as you think of him, but destiny..."

This may be true about destiny but I am a firm believer that God has the last say and He can redeem our destinies for us because His plans for us are good as it is written in the scripture:

For I know the thoughts that I think toward you, says the Lord, thoughts of peace and not of evil, to give you a future and a hope (Jer 29:11).

This story was born out of the redemption of a family for the sake of our fathers, both heavenly and earthly, who endured loneliness without their children.

Chapter 8. In Search of My Dad

By 1987 I had already graduated from high school and was in the workforce. I thought of my dad often but I didn't know how to find him.

"Don't you want to find your dad?" my mom's older sister asked me out of the blue. I lost track of him several years earlier. Even the apartment building we had lived in had been condemned and demolished. A sadness would envelope me whenever I rode the #24 city bus down Genesee Street to work passing my old neighborhood. The building was gone. My dad was gone. My aunt had a great idea.

"Let us go to the Social Security Administration (SSA) in downtown Buffalo and ask them if they can send him a letter if he's still alive."

She knew that as of this time, he was over 62, the age of retirement. Together we found the office and we approached one of the clerks to find out if they could tell us where he was.

"Can you forward a letter to him?" my aunt asked. We waited while she looked up his information. I held my breath wondering if he was still alive knowing if the payments had ceased, I would have my answer.

The clerk indicated that he was still collecting his monthly pension check but she could not give us his address for privacy reasons.

"Yes," she said so I hurriedly wrote a letter stating that I missed him and I was looking for him. What do you say to the dad you haven't seen in almost a decade? We waited a few months, but received no reply. Again, my aunt and I returned to the downtown Social Security Administration office. This time we were told they were willing to send one more letter but if they sent more, it could be considered harassment because he may not want to communicate with me. It was the final letter they sent. I wrote again and we waited for months. I prayed asking God if He would help me, I wouldn't ask for another thing. There was nothing I wanted more than word from my dad wherever he was.

Then one day in 1988 my aunt called me at work. I remember exactly where I was when I took that call. She was clearly excited because she received a letter from my father addressed to me. When we approached the SSA, we had used my aunt's return address. At the time, I still lived home with my mom and adoptive-dad. My aunt was afraid that they would get upset with her if they knew she was helping me find my birth dad. She knew my step-dad had spent a lot of money to adopt me. She was ecstatic and asked if she could open the letter. I could see her smile through the telephone as she described the contents; a beautiful hand-written letter on quality paper, a small Christmas card and a photo of him with his family. We could not decipher a single word. He was in Bulgaria and the letter was hand-written entirely in Cyrillic.

That evening on a dark and rainy night on my way home from work, I visited her except that the weather didn't bother me a bit. Together, we figured out how to have the letter translated into English. She had another great idea to call a Macedonian church in Buffalo. The church arranged a gentleman to meet us on Saturday to read the letter. My aunt and I drove to the church and met with both an older gentleman and a young man around my age. Although kind enough to translate the letter, the older man was not overtly friendly. He read the letter to us and as much as I tried to transcribe it as he read, I did not end up with a fully comprehensible letter. Knowing the Bulgarian community in Buffalo was probably very small and close-knit, I was afraid to call the church again to get another translation.

As the years passed, I no longer remembered what the letter said. I only knew that it was written by my oldest sister, Anelia, on behalf of my father, Peter, and that she had a daughter, Boyana, and two grandsons, Boyko and Simeon. The ages of the grandsons were within a decade of my own age and I longed to meet them. Once again, I found myself searching for another translator. This letter, preserved in a plastic sleeve, became my prized possession. It was the only thing I had left from my dad. Even if I couldn't remember exactly what it said, it reassured me that they truly are my family.

Unanswered Mail

In the late 1980's, I went to the United States Bankruptcy Court for the Western District of New York every afternoon to obtain all the bankruptcy records for the day. They were part of the title work that needed to be done in the business I worked in. On the ground floor was the main post office for the city's downtown region. I would see all the different United States Postal Service forms on the counter as I caught the elevator. They had a variety of postage stamps and forms. There were so many selections to choose from: certified mail, registered mail, airmail, international mail, etc. In seeing all these forms, I approached the postmaster and asked how to mail a letter to Bulgaria explaining I needed proof when it was delivered to the addressee. I wrote a letter of reply to my family addressed to my father, sister and family. The postmaster suggested I send it international registered mail with a return receipt.

Over time, I received the green returned receipt signed in Cyrillic but no written letter in reply. I assumed that since my father was old, he must have died. It didn't stop me from writing though. After all, my sister said they wanted to know what my life was like in the United States of America and I wanted to tell them. Since it was dad's wish that I would not forget him, I was standing on my promise. I sent pictures of my favorite beach in Florida. I sent the sonogram image of my son when I was pregnant. When my son was four, I included photos of us in Niagara Falls. My son grew and another decade passed with no response. Unknown to me at the time, my Bulgarian family was also growing.

A Written Translation

Once again, I searched for a Bulgarian translator in 1999. This time I looked for someone who could take a copy of my father's letter and transcribe it word for word. I asked a friend of mine from South America where he thought I could get a letter translated thinking he might know an international organization. Having been to the University at Buffalo, he suggested I call a lady named Corrine. I called her and asked if they had anyone who could speak Bulgarian.

"No, we don't have any Bulgarians registered on the campus at this time. Give me your name and number and for all I know a Bulgarian could walk into my office this afternoon" Corinne said. She had compassion for my endeavor. Imagine her surprise when what she spoke actually happened! Within a few hours of my call, two Bulgarian men stopped in her office that very afternoon; an uncle and his nephew. The older gentleman was named Rangel and they were there to inquire about English lessons for the young man named Stefan. She called me right after they left her office to say the men took my phone number and they promised to call soon. They did not call that day and I went home disappointed.

The next day though, I heard my name paged on the intercom at work. As soon as I took the call in the lobby, I could tell by the accent that the caller was Bulgarian. The way the caller spoke my name was with the same accent as my dad. The young man on the phone was looking to learn English. He wanted to help me and he could read the letter but he wasn't confident that he could provide the written English translation. Hence the reason he was at the University; to learn how to write English. He inquired of my story and asked for my father's name. As I spoke it in English without the proper Bulgarian pronunciation, he asked me to spell it. He repeated the name to his Uncle Rangel. His uncle actually recognized dad's name!

Rangel, had just returned from Bulgaria a few days earlier and was concerned for Bulgaria with its proximity to the war going on in Kosovo. He explained that they could hear the bombs exploding from Sofia, a little over 200 miles from the border. He said it was a dangerous time in that part of Eastern Europe. My heart ached for Kosovo and my family, wherever and whomever they were. He told me that my father was deceased and I couldn't help but to feel heart-broken.

Rangel said that there was another Bulgarian man in Buffalo who knew my father well. He gave me this gentleman's name as Ivan and went on to say he owned a shop south of Buffalo. These two Bulgarian men became another link in the chain of events that would lead me to finding out where my dad came from and what kind of person he was. Unfortunately, I was still no closer to having my letter translated and dad was dead and no one could bring him back.

I never spoke with Rangel or Stefan again but the saga continued and I was only so grateful for their information.

In April of 1999, I worked for a Canadian firm with several offices globally. I asked a man who knew many people within the organization if there were any Bulgarians working for the company. Surely there was and he found such a man in Montreal named Nikola. Nikola translated the letter and returned it to me in English via e-mail within a day. I could not thank him enough. After that, I could read the letter and cherish its words forever. The original Cyrillic letter was always my prized possession but this English version is what I still read today.

Chapter 9. An Unexpected Connection

I searched for the phone number of the shop owned by Ivan, as suggested by Rangel in 1999. He wasn't a real uncle but considering his close friendship with my dad, he was like a younger brother to him. I arranged a meeting with "Uncle" Ivan at his store for the following Saturday. I went alone. I told him on the phone that I resembled my dad but to my dismay, with my blonde hair and light eyes, he didn't think I looked Bulgarian at all. I only wished I had.

We walked to his private office in the front of the store, closed the door and talked about my dad without interruption for almost two hours. I gave him a copy of the letter and photo to prove who I was. Ivan said he visited him at the greenhouse in the 1970's and saw a young blonde girl there with her mother and grandmother. When Ivan asked who she was, dad said,

"That's her daughter," while pointing to my mother.

He never said I was *his* daughter. Maybe in his own mind after experiencing the tortures of Communism, he feared for my own safety. He was very guarded. We do not know why my father answered him this way but Ivan suggested maybe dad was embarrassed because my mom was so much younger than him. This was only his opinion and I didn't let it bother me.

In the little office, Ivan told me about his wife and children. He had a lot of pride for his store and explained how his children helped with the family business. His wife was educated as a teacher at the University of Buffalo. She was a Macedonian, whom he loved and they had a good marriage. He spoke fondly of his family and Bulgaria. He explained the difficulties that the Bulgarian people were facing at the time. The economy was horrible. It made me wonder how my family was fairing. I was so concerned about them and he said that the next time he visited Bulgaria he would inquire about them.

At the time Ivan met my father, he was a young man about 18 years old. Although both he and my father were born in the same country, they were from different cities. He left Bulgaria for fear of his future and made his way to Greece in the mid 1950's. My dad was about 46 years of age when they met. He met my dad at the mechanical training school in Greece. As previously mentioned, they were both sponsored by the same man, Bogdan Vazov.

With great emotion, Ivan said dad saved his life in Athens. I don't know what kind of school this was because I heard the story many years later. They attended the school for about four months and there was always something disreputable going on. There were about 80 men enrolled in the school and at this time it was a critical situation with the Communists. They were all in Athens awaiting to be admitted into a country that would accept them. According to his memory, some of the nationalities of men in the school were comprised of four Bulgarians (dad and Ivan and the two who were killed), two Croatians, two Serbs, two Yugoslavians and one Macedonian. My dad was a sort of father-figure to Ivan, who was only a young man at the time, giving him advice to help keep him out of trouble, away from fights. He explained that if a man was caught fighting, he would be jailed and no Green Card would be permitted.

While they were at the school, they met a man who was known as a trouble-maker. He told Ivan that once a month a fleet from the USA docked nearby staying a number of days before launching back out to sea. He tried talking Ivan into escaping Athens and stowing away in the ship to sail to the United States of America (USA), entering as an illegal immigrant. My dad discouraged him from doing this and suggested he turn the trouble-maker into the authorities before the law was broken. My dad was concerned that this man would lie and blame the attempted escape on Ivan suggesting it was his idea and he could be arrested and jailed. This was a time of much suspicion and mistrust.

Ivan told me that prior to my dad's final return to Bulgaria in 1981, he tried to fly to Sofia but as he put it, dad got "cold feet" when he landed in Yugoslavia to make his connecting flight. He decided to turn around and return to New York. Once he was back in New York, as he was driving in the City of Buffalo, he accidentally hit a stray dog who ran into the road, injuring it. He scooped up the dog, nursed it back to health and showed up at Ivan's home in the rolling hills of the countryside asking him to keep the dog on his land. Dad was planning once again to attempt to return to Bulgaria and had no space for the dog living in the city. Ivan did not take the dog, saying he already had one.

Then he told me about Bogdan Vazov, their sponsor. As of the time I interviewed Ivan in 1999, he and his family had attended Bogdan's 90th birthday party. Bogdan's son stated that they would all be in attendance at his 100th birthday too, God willing. They very much wanted to celebrate the life of this selfless man. Bogdan lived to the age of 92. He was already deceased by the time I met Ivan so I was not able to meet him. I may have possibly met him as a child but don't remember him. Ivan said that Bogdan's son was a physician in California and his daughter was an architect.

From Ivan's recollection, when no one had heard from my dad in a while and went missing, Bogdan went to the Federal Bureau of Investigations (FBI) looking for him. They told him that someone would have needed to report dad as missing in order to do anything. No one had. Therefore, they could not help him. Bogdan then checked with the Social Security Administration and found out dad had moved to an apartment on Grant Street in Buffalo where he visited him. How Bogdan was given the information freely while I was not, I will never know. This was the same flower shop on Grant Street that I remembered seeing my dad for the last time around 1978, his last known residence in New York State.

Ivan said that my father told Bogdan that he wanted to return to his family in his motherland. So, Bogdan once again took it upon himself to help. Around 1981, Bogdan traveled from Buffalo to Bulgaria to my family's village. He knocked on the door where my brother lived with his family to ask him if he would accept dad back into his life. This was the same homestead my dad reluctantly left a quarter of a century earlier without even hugging his 14-year-old son goodbye. It seemed that in 1981 history repeated itself as my dad left my country without saying goodbye. Just like my brother, I was 14.

As the story was told to me by my niece, Rositsa, she remembered that day very well. Bogdan spoke to my brother for a few hours and they cried together. My brother was so excited that day that he was not himself. My sister-in-law, Ekaterina, was the usual silent and pragmatic partner for she saw the pain and loss her husband experienced the years leading up to this visit. Rositsa only spoke to Mr. Vazov for a few minutes but she understood right away that he was a noble and kind man. At this time, dad was in his early 70's.

Soon after my brother said "Yes," my father landed in Sofia ready to face the last decade of his life still under Communism, although weaker than when he left. The next eight years he spent trying to repair relationships with his estranged wife, three daughters, one son and extended family and tried to enjoy life as best as he could. I can only imagine after leaving them in such dire circumstances 30 years earlier how difficult this must have been. I spent the next 29 years looking for the same family. As I left Ivan's office, with the great pride he instilled in me, he said that I should be proud to be Bulgarian. He believed dad was an honorable man and I was content in this. Yet I was no closer to finding this family.

Chapter 10. It's a Small World

A lthough not as large as Chicago or Toronto, Buffalo has a good number of Bulgarians for a small city. Thanks to sponsors like Mr. Vazov, the small group of men grew into a tight-knit community of immigrants. After my dad and I were separated, any connection with the Bulgarian community came to an end until I met Olga from Pleven in 2002. I mentioned to a coworker that I had Bulgarian roots and she told me there was a Bulgarian lady working there. Olga was out of the office on disability due to a knee injury. For about six weeks, I looked forward to meeting her. Upon her return, we developed a friendship lasting to this day. She is one of the most fascinating people I have ever met and she makes it a point to meet every Bulgarian who comes to Buffalo. Or at least, it seems this way because she knows everyone.

Olga continues to invite me to Bulgarian functions and has introduced me to wonderful ladies who I now call friends. Every spring she sponsors a ladies' tea at her own home and we meet new immigrants. One year, she invited my husband and me to a church picnic. The pastor of her congregation had been to Bulgaria and had made a connection with a local church where she was born. He appreciated the Bulgarian culture and agreed to host a party for the local Bulgarians. Olga urged me to come and meet them too. Without knowing anyone, my husband and I tried to fit in. What a pleasant surprise it was when Ivan and his wife arrived. We had a wonderful afternoon of fun, food and fellowship together.

It is a small world. This is especially true in Buffalo. Around 2004, my husband and I attended a wedding for my husband's step-niece, Michelle. Wouldn't you know it, Ivan and his wife were in attendance. It turned out that Michelle's husband worked for Ivan at his business for years. How wonderful it was to see them again.

In 2016, Olga invited me to another picnic where by chance I met Ivan's niece. The invitation we received had the park shelter number written on it. We found a picnic table under the shelter reserved by the Bulgarians and sat at it awaiting our friends. Some people I had never met were already there and because they didn't know us, they thought we were lost. They politely stated that this was the Bulgarian event and urged us to find our correct party. I explained that I have Bulgarian roots and that my father was one of the original Bulgarians who arrived in Buffalo in the 1950's. They were surprised and very welcoming after hearing this. Since I didn't speak the language, there was a bit of a barrier, but once it was time to eat, that uncertainty went away. They insisted on feeding us whatever they brought. They scooped cucumber and tomato salad and grilled sausages onto our plates and offered us their own distilled spirits called *rakiya*. Eventually, our friends arrived and it was time to dance the *horo*. Originating in the Balkans, this dance is performed as a group linked together, arm in arm. This was the day I met Ivan's niece for the first time.

Maria, a classy and beautiful brunette, lingered longer than just a casual conversation. As we started talking about my dad's history, there was something special about her. She was truly interested in my story and seemed happy that I longed to visit her motherland. She mentioned that as a Bulgarian, her uncle spoiled her and she adored him. He loved her like his own daughter and vowed to bring her to the United States of America over 20 years ago. Like many others, she was awarded a Green Card through the immigration lottery system.

What interested me about Maria was that she explained that she didn't just win the immigration lottery, she prayed for it; declaring it for her children while they still lived overseas. God answered her prayers. The faith and hope she exhibited encouraged me. She came to the United States of America legally. Her uncle was well able to sponsor her and her two children.

Somehow, we stumbled upon her uncle's first name and I realized that her uncle is dad's long-time friend, Ivan. This confirmed what a small world Buffalo really is. Within a week, she invited me to her uncle's home in the rolling hills where they were having a Sunday get together with friends and family. Evidently, they do this often on Sundays especially in the summer.

When we arrived, Maria was in the kitchen preparing food for the party. As we entered the beautiful back yard, I introduced myself to her uncle and his friends. Knowing Ivan did not immediately recognize me since he hadn't seen me in over ten years, I asked him, "Do you know who I am?" He looked puzzled and when I told him whose daughter I am, immediately his eyes welled up with tears. He hugged me and was so happy to see me. Ivan's grandson ran into the kitchen.

"Who is that lady? Grandpa is crying!" He asked his mom. She explained that I am the daughter of a long-time friend. This was a friendship that transcended not only continents but generations too. It was a memorable day as Ivan found it in his heart to tell us additional stories about dad that I hadn't already heard. I met a family who was heading to Sofia that very Fall. They encouraged me to spend time in Sofia, their city of birth.

That year, Ivan turned 80 and lost his beloved wife to cancer. To him, family is everything. He spends his retirement days tending his sumptuous Bulgarian-style garden with the largest, ripest tomatoes you can imagine. His yard is complete with a traditional brick oven like you'd see in the old countries like Bulgaria and Italy. They served traditional Bulgarian cuisine which was a lot like Greek food with a roasted lamb and moussaka with Béchamel sauce. The guests were already swimming in a luxurious in-ground swimming pool. Very nicely landscaped with decorative rocks and benches, the backyard was a bit of an oasis in the valley of the hills. He happily drove his family and friends around on his golf cart passing the grazing animals. He had several acres and I can only imagine how much dad must have admired his home and the beauty surrounding it. It's been over four decades since dad visited there. I explained to Ivan that I found my family and he once again encouraged me to visit his country of birth. He said that most of his family is already in the United States of America or are now deceased.

As the day wore on and more family arrived, the sun started to set over the hills. The reflection of the golden sun on the shimmering water took me to a place somewhere in the universe that seemed to foreshadow my future. I envisioned a place in the old world with rolling hills, sunsets, lakes and mountains. This resembled an ancient land that I couldn't wait to explore with fellow kin I had not yet met.

PART III

JOURNEY TO BULGARIA

Chapter 11. Family Trees

F amily trees come in all shapes and sizes. I have seen some incredibly intricate family trees. Some are constructed in the shape of trees with decorative ornaments, photo books with fancy fonts, Microsoft Word documents and Excel spreadsheets. They can be beautiful hand-drawn trees with names sketched into the branches. As for my attempt, I once piped melted chocolate in the shape of a tree to signify my mother's family onto her 60th birthday cake. If I had attempted before 2016 to do the same for my father's side of the family, it would have been a tree with a single lonesome leaf.

Genealogy

Years ago, I started researching my father's genealogy online using many searches including the website Ancestry.com®. The initial search turned up short given the lack of records. After all, my father had been the first and only person of his family to relocate to the United States of America. In order to research records abroad, I needed to subscribe to a more expensive version of the software. I purchased a subscription and did my best to tackle any Bulgarian documents I came across. I still made no progress and it was disheartening. Since I had already paid the fee, I started doing genealogy for my husband's family, my mom's family and others. I made great strides in filling out the leaves in those trees though my father's tree remained bare. I liked how the software was comprehensive in that the database continued to search for clues related to the information in the family tree, returning possible leads for further investigation even after I logged out of the software. Each lead appeared like a new sprouted leaf.

In the summer of 2015, I began to wonder whether there was anyone in my father's family left in Bulgaria who might want to meet me even if I had not heard from them. The faces in dad's family photo from 25 years earlier came to mind. Did they remember me?

Was it possible that they didn't even know I existed? I had so many unanswered questions and it fueled my drive once more.

Olga had once told me that my father's last name was somewhat uncommon in Bulgaria. It was certainly not the equivalent of Smith or Jones in the United States of America. At a loss, at the advice of something I read online, I tried dividing his name into two words. I wondered if the name may have had French roots. That led me nowhere. Another variation of his name led me to a sizeable Jewish immigrant community in - surprisingly - Bermuda. A blood test I had in 2008 revealed that there was Jewish descent in my lineage but I didn't know by which parent. I checked Jewish genealogical records on JewishGen.org with no success. I also checked names from the Holocaust and there were no matches.

There was a funeral director by a last name similar to my birth name in New Jersey serving the Jewish community so I reached out to her. As far as the funeral director knew, her family was not Jewish but she did have ancestors in the United Kingdom including a distant relative buried at Westminster Abbey. Could we all be descended from some prominent figure from England? In 2012, I ordered a book from Amazon titled "The [Avramov] Name in History" and all I could find was that the name had roots in England. I even found a record on Ancestry.com® of a man with the exact same last name as my dad who immigrated to Cuba around the same time he immigrated to the United States of America. They all proved to be dead ends. My hunt turned to Facebook where I searched every possible phonetic spelling of my father's name. Some profiles had similar names but none were related.

On Thanksgiving Day of 2015, the realization that I may never find my dad's family hit me and I felt sad. After preparing and cooking the meal, the holiday festivities and traditional meal had ended. I sat relaxing enjoying dessert and coffee with a close friend who spent the holiday with us and helped clean up after dinner. I spoke with her about my concern and she suggested we pray about it. I had prayed before to find my dad's family and was filled with so much hope. I felt that I had exhausted my search. I was losing hope. As it is written in the scripture:

Hope deferred makes the heart sick, But when the desire comes, it is a tree of life (Prov 13:12).

My friend suggested I lay this burden at the foot of the Cross of Jesus and we prayed together that God's will would be done. As it is written in the scripture:

God sets the solitary in families; He brings out those who are bound into prosperity; But the rebellious dwell in a dry land (Ps 68:6).

We agreed that if it was God's will that I would find them, then it would indeed happen. I have since pondered the idea of surrendering. When we "let go and let God," do we allow God to move on our behalf? I believe so. I only wonder why I hadn't laid the burden down sooner. Was it an obedience thing? Was it a timing thing? It was God's time.

A few weeks passed and Thanksgiving turned into Christmas and amidst all the Christmas cards in the mail I received a coupon for 50% off an Ancestry.com® membership. This was the first time I had received such a coupon from Ancestry.com® and I thought it was odd. I immediately thought of my husband's sister, who always shared the most delightful family stories, and how we could research her genealogy on their next visit to Buffalo. This would occur around my husband's birthday. I filed the coupon away but pondered the idea of renewing my subscription using the coupon after the holidays. I wanted to wait until I had more time to devote to the hobby. The only problem was that the coupon was good for the domestic version not the international version of the software. The domestic version would not help me with my Bulgarian search but I could continue building trees for others.

Around the same time, I received an e-mail from someone inquiring about my husband's great-grandfather with the surname Casagrande - which means "big house" - from Venice. This person had an Ancestry.com® account but he was asking for access to my husband's family tree which I had set to "private." With my husband's permission, I replied and granted him full access.

The same day I replied to the Casagrande request, I decided to open my own [Avramov] family tree which had laid dormant due to the dead end I had reached. I don't even know why I opened it except that God had ordered my steps. As it is written in the scripture:

The steps of a good man are ordered by the Lord, And He delights in his way (Ps 37:23).

End of the Drought

Imagine my surprise when I saw a single new leaf indicating a new hint of a possible new lead. Had I not gone onto the website to help the Casagrande descendant, I would never have come across this new lead of my own. I opened the leaf and it contained information I already knew such as dad's date of death, but it stated that he died in Sofia. I had always surmised that he died in the village where he lived. It is true, dad did not die in Sofia. The record only stated as such because as the capital, all records go through Sofia. It was enough to catch my attention knowing it was a record I had never seen. I looked at the user's name and it was one I did not recognize. I wondered if this new leaf was a possible distant relative. Indeed, the new leaf was a new lead! What a coincidence that both of us had built our own tree with a solitary leaf containing the same single ancestor.

The same way I had contacted the Casagrande user to give them access to my husband's family tree, I did so with this new lead. I didn't know where they were located but they surprised me by replying right away! They requested the name of my father's village so we could determine if we had a common relative. When I mentioned the name of the village, it was a match. We were both stunned and ecstatic. The owner of this leaf turned out to be my great-nephew, Momchil, and I learned that he is the grandson of Tanya, one of my three Bulgarian sisters. At the time, Tanya was still alive. I requested information regarding our family tree and away Momchil went building the tree. Where I had reached a dead end, it took him only a few weeks to build. It seemed that those two weeks were the longest of my life. When I didn't hear from him, I figured he must have thought I was some kind of internet stalker and decided not to reply.

Once again, I prayed that God would work on my behalf and prove to Momchil who I was. It took 13 days to be exact for him to reply with all the names of my immediate family - my very large family!

This new information made me quickly forget about the "Ancestry leaf drought." His records showed three sisters and one brother and nineteen descendants – including four generations of relatives. He wrote the year of birth next to each name. The intricate family tree that I had longed for was already built and for this reason, he is special to me. My sister, Tanya, was instrumental in her grandson reaching out to Ancestry.com®. Years ago, she gave him our father's social security number. This information is what triggered a leaf to appear on my family tree. Although gone now to be with the Lord, Tanya leaves behind an amazing legacy through three generations.

As thrilled as I was about the quantity of family, I was even more concerned about how each and every person was doing.

"How is the family?" I inquired.

"Great!" Momchil replied.

That one little word equally made my heart soar and made me all the more ravenous for additional information. Who were they and how could I get to know them? As the weeks passed, I asked him to have his mother, Elena, 'friend request' me on Facebook so I could communicate with her. It was more appropriate and comfortable that way because my great-nephew is around the same age as my own son, Jacob. Elena and I quickly became acquainted and communicated by both e-mail and Facebook messenger. She sent me pictures of my sister, although aged with her health failing. I could tell Elena was a very loving daughter-in-law to my sister and this made me happy. I saw photos of her husband, Alexander, who reminded me so much of dad. Even photos of Momchil resembled my son.

It was from Elena that I learned that my brother, Vasil, had died suddenly in 1998. When he died, our name literally died with him. It finally made sense why it was so hard to find any current information on my dad's last name. No other males with my father's last name existed within our family. The only Bulgarian siblings I have left are female. Dad would be proud and quite surprised at how many boys the family currently has. Unless my son has a daughter in the future, Tatiana, my great-niece, will be the only girl in her generation.

A few months later, Elena contacted her husband's cousin in my family's village to tell her they found me. Although they live only a few hours apart, Elena lives in the capital and Rositsa near the 2nd largest city in Bulgaria, Plovdiv. Elena's mother-in-law, Tanya, and most of my family including Rositsa live within walking distance of each other.

Elena later told me that they actually won a Green Card through the immigration lottery in the 1990's but because she had recently lost one of her parents and she was pregnant with one of the boys, they chose to decline the opportunity and remain with their family. They didn't know anyone in the United States of America. Surely their newfound relative was causing a stir in the family.

Chapter 12. The Love of a Brother

Although I never met my brother because he was already deceased, I felt his love through his daughter, Rositsa. She lives with her family on the land dad left behind. The relationship with this branch started a few months after I found Momchil on Ancestry.com®. Rositsa was quite surprised by the connection the family in Sofia had made with me.

"Whose daughter, are you?" I asked. I was thrilled to learn that she's my brother's daughter, an only child. Hearing the news that they found me caused so much excitement for Rositsa, that she could not sleep. It would unfold early in our relationship that a letter I addressed to my father with the photos of my son in the late 1990's was in her possession. The letter was delivered to her home previously belonging to my brother. By the time she came across my letter, dad had been dead for ten years. My letter gave her a glimmer of hope of an extended family. Without any of my letters being returned, I continued to think that someone was reading my letters, although they were being sent to my oldest sister. My hope was a reality. We realized that we were living somewhat parallel lives. With the aid of the computer's translator, Google Translate, we got to know each other very well. Although all the words didn't translate perfectly, we didn't sweat the small stuff.

Our budding relationship became her opportunity to make up for lost time. At the time she found one of my letters 20 years earlier, her father had recently passed away and she was mourning the loss of both of our fathers. As time went by, life went on and she raised her children at the same time I raised my son. We realized that we were both pregnant with our boys at the same time. What a coincidence in that we feel that the children are extraordinary like their grandparents and their resemblance is quite amazing. My son resembles my father while her son resembles her father.

After connecting on Facebook, we then communicated by e-mail including longer letters. I learned that my widowed sister-in-law, Ekaterina, lives with her. As the weeks and months of 2016 passed,

Rositsa and I became closer sometimes writing daily and at other times checking in with each other weekly. If a few weeks or month went by with no communication, we worried.

A librarian by trade, Rositsa loved books as much as I did and we talked about the libraries in our cities. She also yearned to write a book about our family. Together we started dreaming about the day we would meet. We realized how we were raised similarly and we had the same personality traits. We became the dreamers with the hope of a family reunification and restoration of our family name. This would be for an appointed time as it is written in the scripture:

For the vision is yet for an appointed time; But at the end it will speak, and it will not lie. Though it tarries, wait for it; Because it will surely come, It will not tarry (Hab 2:3).

We never let our distance or language get in the way. We discussed how we both love movies and she encouraged me to watch films with English subtitles such as "The World is Big and Salvation Lurks Around the Corner." We wrote about the lives of noteworthy Bulgarians. She spoke of writers like Ilija Trojanow. We talked about our intent of telling the world about our encouraging story of the redemption of a family torn apart by Communism brought together by a naïve American separated by distance and language through our own media. We dreamed of travelling through Europe and even discussed one day visiting Paris and Rome together.

In the Spring of 2016, I went to dinner at Olga's house to help us prepare for our trip abroad. Except for myself, all the women in attendance were native Bulgarians while our husbands were born in the USA. Olga figured this way my husband could mingle with the men and get comfortable with the idea of traveling there. All the men had been to Bulgaria with their wives.

There, I met a lady named Polina who was about to travel to Plovdiv to visit her family in a few weeks where both of our families reside. She invited me to travel with her but my instincts told me it was too soon to meet my long-lost family. Timing - God's timing - is everything. As it is written in the scripture:

To everything there is a season, A time for every purpose under heaven (Eccl 3:1).

I still needed time to develop a relationship with them for we were still strangers. That was a tough decision for me because I wanted to be impulsive and go with Polina, but who would I stay with? I didn't know her well enough to stay at her parents' home. I also didn't know the language and had yet to fully correspond with Rositsa as I had just connected with my niece only a week earlier. She connected with Polina on Facebook.

When Rositsa learned that Polina had visited her own city without getting the chance to meet her, she was upset with me. I had a hard time explaining why I hadn't mentioned that she was arriving in our conversations. This caused me to rewrite my words several times hoping Google Translate would get my message and tone correct. It was so important to me to preserve this new relationship I was establishing and it was complicated but she forgave me. Google Translate was new to me and it was the only way we could communicate but I refused to let that incident hinder me from fostering a strong relationship with Rositsa.

As 2016 passed and I got to know more of the family, we developed a trust for one another. Over the course of the year we wrote often, discussing historical events that occurred with the family. We plotted out the trip we would take when we visited for the first time. We shared funny stories about dad. We shared things we both experienced with him even though he was in our lives at different stages; her in her early twenties and me the first seven years of my life. I was happy that she had seen my father more recently than I had because it brought us closer together. She had information I needed. My father raised her dad, Vasil, until he left Bulgaria when my brother was around 14. Vasil raised her with the same family values he was taught.

One of the memories we discussed was that dad had shipped her a doll as a gift while he was with me in Buffalo in the 1970's.

"For Christmas I get strange gifts that come from afar. The packages are so fragmented, and the stuff inside so broken, that the doll is almost barefoot. Even the huge chocolate rabbit is just a bunch of crumbs with a loose ribbon and one ear." Rositsa recalls. We realized that we had the same type of dolls, possibly purchased together and we immediately felt like sisters. Although I was her aunt, younger by seven years, I was like the sister she had always prayed for and we couldn't have been happier.

Rositsa was a young adult when she discovered the truth about the family. In 1979, as a runner, she was denied a visa to travel from the train station in Plovdiv to West Germany with a team of athletes for political reasons. When she asked her father why this was so, she only got half the story. A similar thing occurred with Momchil's dad who was in the military academy. Because of the history of their grandfather, they were denied opportunities due to his dossier. This was the way with the Communists. Thankfully, time has healed these wounds and I am proud of my niece and nephew's resilience.

Rositsa played a role in assisting dad to retain his citizenship when he returned around 1980. There was a new amnesty program for political prisoners to return to Bulgaria but it was a new and complex process. She lived a few hours from the capital and had to do all the research and legwork to arrange the proper paperwork. It was almost denied. Thankfully she persevered for his sake and his citizenship was reinstated. When he first arrived, she was about 20 years old, a youth full of energy. Still today, she continues to dig into the records of the State Archives for information on dad's arrest. She recently discovered that his arrest date was May 17, 1951 and that he was accused of being a member of an illegal organization opposed to the Bulgarian Communist Party. Neither of us are sure of the accuracy of this claim.

After he returned to Bulgaria, dad lived with my brother and his family. From what I could gather, he took turns living with all of his children at one time or another during the 1980's. During that period, Rositsa worked for a shoe factory. Dad woke up early and over time a simple thing he taught her was how to brew a good, strong cup of coffee. They enjoyed coffee together just as dad and I had as a child. Even today, although an ocean apart, we laugh as Rositsa and I take coffee breaks together swapping photos of our coffee cups. We don't need to speak the same language to enjoy a good, strong cup of coffee like dad taught us.

As 2016 passed, Rositsa described many of the Bulgarian holidays sending long e-mails explaining the history and purpose of the holidays. I could tell she was a librarian. Her favorite holiday was the day celebrated May 24th for Saints Cyril and Methodius, two Byzantine Christian brothers who were credited with the development of the Glagolitic alphabet. She shipped me a language book hoping I would grasp her mother tongue. Many people believe that the Cyrillic alphabet originated in Russia but it was actually developed by Bulgarian students of these two brothers. The holiday is a day of celebration for anyone involved in education in Bulgaria. As a worker in a prominent school in Plovdiv, she always celebrates the holiday with great joy and in 2017 we were together when the holiday arrived.

Both the Eastern Orthodox and Christian Easter holidays fell on the same day in 2016 which is rare. Rositsa and I decided to shift to Skype. Although Momchil offered to translate for us, I didn't want to inconvenience him as he lives two hours from Rositsa. We Skyped with her daughter, Tatiana, and my American niece, Elizabeth, as they taught us how to color eggs, the Bulgarian way at Easter. We worked without talking. The activity was more of a learn by doing anyway. The results were beautiful one-of-a-kind egg designs resembling tie-dye. These were the eggs Elizabeth and I shared with our American family for Easter. During this time, Rositsa presented a gift of beautiful cream-colored hand knit socks that Ekaterina had made for Elizabeth and her mother, Anastasia. After arriving in Bulgaria, the next month Ekaterina gave me the socks for the girls and Elena, gave me a half dozen ornate Easter eggs to take home, but these were to admire not to eat.

Around this time, Rositsa's kittens were born and I couldn't wait to meet the litter of two; one orange and one brown calico. Five weeks later we would all be together in person on my long-awaited trip to Bulgaria where my relatives including the kittens would embrace me for the first time as one of their own. What a joy it was.

Chapter 13. Journey to the Old World

The first time I ever considered going to Bulgaria was in 1988 upon receipt of my father's letter. I longed to visit him and the family but it was difficult to enter a Communist country. There was a language barrier too. At a minimum I needed a passport which I did not obtain until 2008. I would need a visa which I had no guarantee would be approved. The barriers to entry seemed insurmountable. The Berlin Wall was intact and Communism was still the rule of law. The airline tickets were expensive and I would have needed to save up for quite a while to afford to travel that far at that age. When I tried to call them on a landline in 1988, I got disconnected by the telephone operator because I had the wrong phone number. After the initial letter dad sent me, I received no further communication from them.

Over the years my desire to go waned because I knew my dad was dead and I didn't think anyone else knew that I existed. It wasn't until I met Ivan, did he refuel my desire to see his homeland. Even so, it still took me another 18 years to finally make the personal connections and go. Even Olga tried persuading me to go to Bulgaria with her but I knew it wasn't quite the right time yet. My family needed time to plan for our arrival. They had details to work out to host us, time to request off from their jobs, money to save for the excursions and personal schedules to arrange. The itinerary was compact with many places to tour and the timetable was aggressive. We decided that late spring of 2017 would be the best time.

It was Rositsa who planned the 2017 trip from beginning to end with input from Momchil's family. Part of the itinerary was based on the supposed route my dad took with Alexi when they left Bulgaria prior to the summer of 1954 on their way to Greece. The only differences being that we were on holiday and not fleeing for our lives. We drove in nice cars and stayed at boutique hotels while they walked and had no place to lay their heads. Our reunion would be fueled by the two of us who lived in two different worlds searching for the truth about our ancestors; me as the daughter and her as the granddaughter of the same man. Each of us in our own way had endeavored to reach the truth about our family. For my reason was personally motivated and hers was politically.

The month leading up to our arrival, Rositsa visited Momchil's family in Sofia to go over details of our trip. Likewise, Aleksander and Elena visited Rositsa and Marco in the village. Elena sent photos of their meetings and their anticipation of the trip encouraged me. Prior to our trip, we Skyped with Aleksander's family discussing plans for our arrival in Sofia in May of 2017.

I heard rumors that new laws were being passed in my own country regarding the need for Visas but the time was too short for us to obtain them. My family assured me that there would be no need for a Visa. Of course, we would be admitted to Bulgaria as tourists. The Skype meeting brought us much relief. Elena, a lawyer, knew about such things and thankfully Momchil was a great translator.

In Advance, Rositsa and her husband, Marko, visited the hotels we planned to rent during our vacation together. They made the journey through the twists and turns of the rugged landscape in the weeks leading up to our visit. She said that in no uncertain terms would they allow us to rent a car. She insisted that driving in Bulgaria was more difficult than in the United States of America and that it would be too much of a burden for us. We agreed and were very relieved that Aleksander, and occasionally Tatiana, drove us everywhere.

We originally planned on transferring in Europe through Rome and spending a few days in Italy to adjust to the time zone. But about five months prior to our trip, we changed our minds and flew via Austrian Airlines through Vienna. Olga was on the same flight making the trip as far as Vienna to spend a few days touring the capital city with recommendations made by Momchil. He had studied there a few years earlier. This happened to be the destination of our layover before continuing to Sofia.

This was the trip Olga and I spoke about for over ten years. She had a family graduation party to attend in Pleven and we were meeting my family for the first time in Sofia. We both went our separate ways in Vienna but after her tour we would only be a few hours apart if I needed her for any reason.

Touching Down in Sofia

My family was set to meet us at the airport. I slept very little on the overnight flight from New York. We were tired upon landing in Bulgaria but the tiredness did not last long. Knowing I was about to meet the family I had longed to see for decades, excitement had taken over. I remember that we sat near the front of the airplane so we could disembark as soon as possible. The flight attendants were very attentive and it seemed as though the voices of the passengers around us were unusually hushed. There was a peacefulness that enveloped me as we flew through the Balkan territory and landed in Sofia. When we landed, I felt as if I was home, which was odd because I usually only feel this way when I land in Buffalo.

On the first day of our trip to Bulgaria, we made it through the terminal with our carry-ons and backpacks, eventually arriving at the entrance where the travelers are greeted. I had a suitcase packed to the brim with a variety of gifts for my newfound family including flowers I designed and stitched together with green thread. They became a lasting token in their homes after I left with the stems rotating like a children's toy mobile. They reminded me of the flowers my father grew in Buffalo. All of a sudden, I heard someone call out my name and there they were - smiling, waving excitedly and clutching a basket of fresh flowers for me. I couldn't get to them fast enough as I ran down a pedestrian ramp leaving my husband a few steps behind. There was my family; Rositsa, Tatiana, Aleksander and Momchil. They were four family members from two of my deceased siblings. We must have proceeded to pick up our checked baggage but I hardly remember that. I was so thrilled to be in the land of my ancestors.

As we walked through the airport, surprisingly we weren't in a hurry to leave. Aleksander asked if we wanted to stop for coffee. Initially I thought he was only being polite. In the States, we would have left the airport immediately, but not today, at least not here. "Enjoy Everyday Life" was printed on Momchil's tee-shirt. This was a different land and a different way of life where we didn't feel the need to rush like New Yorkers. In Plovdiv they have a special phrase for this which I would learn about later on the journey.

After we found a modern but quaint booth to relax, Aleksander ordered coffee for all of us. I chose my favorite drink, a cappuccino, the first of many I would experience with them. I later found that Aleksander made the best cappuccinos at home. My family went on to explain that when they picked my father up from the airport, they had the same tradition. Although the café was not as fancy then, they still made it a point to sit in the airport to enjoy each other's company over a cup of coffee before carrying on their journey to the village. They had waited decades to see our father just as I had waited decades to see them. They wanted to do the same with me as a memorial to my dad.

This was the first of many coffees I would enjoy with such a sentimental bunch. Rositsa explained to me that in 1981, she and her family drove the two-hour journey to meet dad at the airport. Back then, they left their home in the middle of the night and Rositsa was so tired that she left the house in her slippers. They had to turn around and return home to change her shoes. Although only a few-hour drive, her father did not want to be late when the plane arrived and risk missing dad's arrival. While we enjoyed our beverages, Elena was preparing for our arrival at their modern home in the ancient city of Sofia.

After coffee at the airport, we headed to my nephew's home. As we drove through the city, I marveled at the mix of old and new architecture. The Communist era buildings were noticeable but Sofia has her share of modern glass buildings too. The elevated statue of Sofia was more beautiful than I anticipated and we couldn't help but to be in awe of the Vitosha mountains as they rose prominently in the distance. The landscape was very green and reminded me a lot of my home state, New York. After we settled and unpacked, Rositsa and Tatiana arrived and we all enjoyed a full Bulgarian style meal that started with a traditional *shopska salad* with tomatoes, cucumbers and feta cheese as the main ingredients. While still in the United States of America, I was informed by my Bulgarian friends that the first course of the meal could take an hour so to savor it. My friends said the salad is customary. Americans tend to eat their entire meal in less time it takes to eat a *shopska salad*.

My family had the traditional homemade bread called *tutmanik*, a sign of welcome to the house guests. We were invited to break off the first roll from the round baked loaf. Although this was an early meal compared to other large meals we subsequently ate in the evening, it was a full meal of home cooked bread, meats and salads including a fruity vegan style dessert with a strong citrus taste which I loved. The slow cooked meal of beef melted in our mouths. We enjoyed wine and *rakiya* in the peaceful surroundings of the family I could not believe I was with. This first meal along with so many others were surreal.

Aleksander and Elena were amazing hosts in a country that prides itself in hospitality. The culture of the Bulgarians provides the best service to guests as possible. This was stated in travel videos I had watched before visiting the country. I also read that they take this warm welcoming more serious than most countries as if it is a responsibility. Although not surprised, I was very impressed with the care they provided.

The afternoon went fast and it seemed too soon that Rositsa and Tatiana had to depart for the village to finish preparing their home for our arrival the very next day. After our wonderful meal, we spent the early evening in the capital as we briefly acquainted ourselves with the neighborhood of the Church of St. George, and the Aleksander Nevsky Cathedral during the glowing sunlight of the golden hour. St. Sofia Church was recorded as the oldest church in Sofia.

We learned that prior to the Bulgarian National Revival, Russia was a friend to Bulgaria aiding them in the escape and release from the grip of the Ottoman-Turks in the late 1800's. After five centuries, the tide of change came to Bulgaria thanks to Russia stirring a revival that is still evident today. It was a beautiful much needed walk after a long flight and delicious first meal together. They were delightful to be with as we learned the history of this dramatic cathedral shining in the setting sun. After the tour, we retired early and enjoyed a restful evening in the lovely ambiance of Aleksander and Elena's home.

Peaceful Hospitality

While in Bulgaria, Aleksander drove us everywhere. His sons translated for us. They insisted that while we were together, we had one of the young adults who knew English with us. Our interpreters were always kind-hearted, anticipating what we needed. They were patient and respectful even when we exhausted them. They always explained where we were going and what was occurring. We were so grateful to them.

Not only did they give us the best room in the home, they insisted on paying for many of our activities and restaurant meals while together. This was no ordinary family, they arranged all their schedules to be away from work for two full weeks, the entire length of our trip. Whether in Sofia, the family's village or the places we toured, they never left us alone in this foreign country.

On the second day of our trip while still in Sofia, Elena and Aleksander taught me how to make a traditional *banitza*. The main difference between the *banitza* I've had in America versus the traditional one of Bulgaria is in the pastry which is the main ingredient. Here we use eggs, yogurt and feta cheese rolled in phyllo dough and baked, but in Bulgaria they have special dough similar to burrito shells but much thinner and larger in diameter. Their feta cheese was not as salty as some I've eaten at home. They refrigerate the rectangular blocks of cheese in brine when not using it. We made the largest *banitza* I've ever seen baked with real butter and sunflower oil; one of their most abundant seed oils. This delicacy fed seven of us adults with leftovers. This cooking lesson was one of the reasons we were late for our next destination but I learned that you can't rush good cooking.

We were headed to Rositsa's home in the family's village where I was meeting the rest of the family. I was worried because I thought we were late. I don't know how a hostess can handle this when preparing meals serving several courses. Maybe this is the key to the hour-long salad that is served first; awaiting the late guests. Or possibly why they serve dessert in the middle of the afternoon. I fit right in. Not only were we enjoying breakfast full of pastries, yogurt, and my nephew's delicious cappuccino, we were all packing for the two-week family vacation leaving from the village the next morning. After breakfast, we all loaded into two cars and took a leisurely drive to the village where the rest of the family lives. My 17-year-old great-nephew, Radoslav, was still in high school and in the middle of the exam season. So unfortunately, he was left behind for his studies but was able to join us a week later in Plovdiv. Aleksander and his family were kind enough to accommodate us despite Radoslav's schedule which was amazing and we appreciated it.

The hospitality we received at Aleksander's home was phenomenal but it didn't end there. His sister, Violeta, amazed me with the appetizers she served at her dad's home. We packed a lot into the day including the surprise welcome for us by Violeta before heading to Rositsa's.

Chapter 14. Safe in the Family's Village

Unfortunately, five months before my epic trip my middle sister died. We would never meet, at least not in this lifetime. Momchil was the one to break the news to me around Christmas of 2016. The flowers I planned to send for Christmas became flowers of condolences. Tanya wasn't the only one I would never meet. My brother was also dead.

Our first stop was the home of my late sister and brother-in-law, Borislav, along with his dog. They were welcoming us into the village with this first stop by their daughter, Violeta. When I met her, we clung to each other amazed at our physical similarities. Violeta and I made it a point to have our photo taken together overlooking the backyard which has seen many seasons of gardening. Here was the largest yellow rose bush I had ever seen.

Violeta had already prepared a delightful table full of Bulgarian style snacks and beverages but I didn't know, it was a surprise.

"Do you want to stay for a snack?" asked Violeta. Gergana interpreted for us. I hesitated because I thought we were already late to arrive at Rositsa's home. Not knowing the culture, I almost said "No." Then Gergana whispered and said,

"Say Yes!"

Once inside my brother-in-law's home, Violeta had made a traditional homemade bread served with a spiced salt mix for dipping made special for us. I was welcome to take the first piece of bread. All of this was being explained to me by our interpreters, Momchil and Gergana.

In the late afternoon, we said farewell to Violeta, Borislav and Emiliya, one of my great-great-nieces. Aleksander drove us to Rosita's home which was the homestead of my brother a short distance away where we spent the night in my family's village for the first time. Both of my remaining sisters were waiting for my arrival along with their families and they humbled me by their presence. Blagorodna and Anelia are an entire generation older than me. In their own language they said that they never dreamed that I would travel so far to meet them. I never anticipated that they wanted to meet me, their half-sister who is the age of their own children. I was quickly introduced to them then ushered up to our room which overlooked the backyard where they were all gathered.

I had a few minutes to change my clothes. The weather had cooled off a bit from the warmth of the city. Under the canopy of the shady trees and crawling grape vines, Rositsa arranged the tables for at least twenty of us situated on the side of the yard between her home and Blagorodna's. As they were waiting for us, Rositsa had served a delicious homemade yellow marble cake with a meringue frosting and coffee.

We were officially introduced to the family and it was time to share stories about my dad's life with them after he had arrived in 1981. Meeting them in the garden sitting around this large group of people knowing they were the people I had searched for felt like a dream. The faces of the people who I stared at in a photo taken decades earlier were looking me in the face. I will always remember the smiles and laughter. This is where Momchil took a group photo of us in front of the privet hedge in Rositsa's yard. It would become the largest of the group photos with all of dad's three daughters together.

It was getting late and I thought we had missed dinner but after my elderly sisters retired for the evening, we started a several-course dinner lasting until almost midnight. Similar to my nephew Aleksander's family, Rositsa took three weeks off of work to prepare for our visit and to spend the full time with us. Her loving care for us in every aspect was such as the love of a brother as it is written in the scripture:

Let brotherly love continue. Do not forget to entertain strangers, for by so doing some have unwittingly entertained angels (Heb 13:1-2).

Blagorodna's home is adjacent to Rositsa's. Her residence houses four generations. She resides in the main home with her husband, Mikhail. My niece, Janeta, lives there with her husband, Emil. My great nephew, Stoyko, also lives there with his adorable wife, Mariela, and young son, Tosho.

What surprised me the most about Blagorodna's family was the sheer joy on their faces in meeting us and how they couldn't get enough of us. They were unable to travel with us for the next week but they wanted to get to know us more. They didn't have the year of preparation or the letters that the others had. They had only been prepped a month or so before our trip and until the last minute, I was not sure I would meet them.

Friendly Neighbors, Friendly Family

Every morning I was so happy to hear Mariela shout from the side door a welcoming "hello" in English as I stepped outside Rositsa's. The joy in her voice and the friendliness of this family was exhilarating. The day after our first meeting, we travelled with Aleksander and Rositsa's families promising that upon our return, we would spend more time with Blagorodna's family.

Prior to our visit, some relatives had never met each other. It seemed odd because they live in a small country, the size of Tennessee. As in any family, there seemed to be circumstances that I didn't understand but I was just a naïve American trying to grasp the family dynamics. I was content enjoying the fact that God was using me to facilitate communication between people who didn't even speak my own language. Uncovering the mystery of the family dynamics was not important to me. Loving them by spending time with them was important. I was certain it was by God's grace that this whole trip had worked out in my favor in the first place. I can surmise that my need to find this family stemmed from an insecurity in myself due to the promise I made to my dad at the age of eleven. The promise prompted me to spend decades of my life yearning to find them but God is the One who places these desires into our hearts as it is written in the scripture:

> *Delight yourself also in the Lord, And He shall give you the desires of your heart (Ps 37:4).*

What if God's time had finally arrived and He was the One who sent me to help heal a family that had been torn apart for a variety of reasons? How better to accomplish this than with a long-lost hopeful American who wanted to meet everyone and learn everything.

Boyko, the oldest grandson of my sister, Anelia, had lasting memories of my father from the 1980's. After looking at photos of us together, I realized that we resemble each other enough to pass for siblings! A young boy himself when my dad arrived, he told us stories that were quite funny. One story in particular was about how dad bragged to his friends in town about how much his Social Security check was worth at the time. Evidently this was a sore subject among the Communists who reprimanded him to not speak on such matters. It was a modest amount in the USA but the value of the dollars in Bulgaria was greater. He continued to repeat this among his friends. Although far from the freedom of the United States of America, he spoke his mind. His boldness became evident and his humor continued with him in his advanced years. Even Boyko's humor reminded me of my own dad's.

The weather became damp and chilly as the day wore on and both of my sisters and their families said their good-byes. We made plans to get back together after returning from our sightseeing trip a week later. I headed into the house and spent some time with Ekaterina, my sister-in-law, in her room with Gergana. This was the same room dad occupied when he lived there in the 1980's. As we sat at a square folding table with a plaid tablecloth sharing stories, Rositsa prepared dinner. I wished I had been able to spend more time with her before dinner but we were assured we would have more time later.

The dinner started with a beautiful beet salad including slices of deliciously roasted ham. The main course included roasted potatoes, beef and chicken and the most delicious mushroom caps filled with melted butter and oil. I enjoyed my time cooking and dining in

Rositsa's home. It was unique in that she has an eat-in kitchen where the food is prepped and cooked. We always ate in my favorite room, the dining room. It was very carefully designed with two long tables and nicely cushioned built-in seating or banquette along the windows. When not relaxing in the dining room, we enjoyed our coffee in the garden. Like my dad, her love of flowers was very evident.

Chapter 15. Family Vacation

On day three of our Bulgarian trip, Rositsa cooked us a breakfast similar to French toast consisting of sliced bread dipped in egg and fried served with Blagorodna's family organic honey. After breakfast, Aleksander and his family arrived and in three cars, nine of us departed on our family holiday. Again, my husband and I rode in Aleksander's car accompanied by Momchil. Elena and Gergana rode with Tatiana. Rositsa and Marco rode in their own car and we all caravanned south towards Asen's Fortress. We drove to the mountains, through the valleys and over some very scary terrain near natural caves on our way to visit several sites. I tried not to get carsick from the twists and turns of the mountain roads so I closed my eyes. We drove so much that at times that I longed to be still but I wasn't there to sit and relax, I was there to visit the home of my ancestors.

Asen's Fortress

One of my favorite places among all of the sites was Asen's Fortress near the Bachkovo Monastery in the Valley of the Thracian Kings a short drive from Plovdiv. This fortress is on a cliff in the Rhodope Mountains very close to the Town of Asenovgrad. It was here that Gergana told us about a stamp booklet containing 100 of the top Bulgarian historical places to visit.

For a mere few Leva we purchased of booklet to collect stamps and at each visit to one of the historical places, we received a special stamp at that site. It made a great souvenir, one that we will bring with us each time we return to Bulgaria in the future. Here, we walked through the small but amazing fortress, a medieval stronghold dating back over 800 years. Some ruins on the property were dated before Christ was born. The fortress contained frescos from at least two different eras that were peeking through the plaster. The frescos were completely covered during the rule of the Ottoman-Turks due to the art's Christian religious nature. In a way the plaster meant to cover the truth of the pictures helped to preserve the inspirational messages hidden beneath. What I liked the most about this fortress were the arched windows and curved walls allowing for light to stream in from the ceiling. It felt like a light from heaven telling us that we were at the right place at the right time.

Momchil and Gergana climbed to a higher stone and sat together enjoying the amazing view of the valley from high up. I was proud to capture their photo while up there with the Bulgarian flag as they were always so photogenic.

Along the climb up to the fortress we chuckled as we saw *martenitsas* hanging on a tree. As an annual tradition, people give these braided red and white strings as bracelets or tassels to each other at the beginning of March. They are worn on wrists or garments for the entire month or until a stork is seen whichever is first. After this time, they are removed and hung on the nearest tree. It is related to *Baba Marta*, a mythical figure. This tradition is passed down from generation to generation promoting health for the year and is a sure sign of spring. The martenitsas had been left there by other passersby the previous month of March. It was a reminder that in the springtime of 1954, dad and Alexi would have passed through these same parts.

Bachkovo Monastery

After descending the cliff near the fortress, we drove a short distance to the Bachkovo Monastery. Bachkovo, like many others in the Christian nation, has a distinctive look with its arches, columns, tiled roofs and frescos. There are so many monasteries in this part of the world. Upon arriving, I noticed that the grounds were very well-manicured. To reach the monastery itself, we passed a sequoia tree whose trunk was so large that four of us could not collectively wrap our arms around it. We entered through a wide stone portico with iron gates. To enter the chapel, we had to step down two feet to its doorway. Once inside, I was impressed with a circular gilded rendering of Jesus on the ceiling. The courtyard, though old with many large inlaid stones had a rectangular grassy area that was well-kept where Momchil, Elena and I sat on a stone wall awaiting the others who were on their own walks through.

Along a pedestrian way to the monastery merchants sell their goods. They were lined up on both sides and I wish I had browsed longer to purchase their handicrafts ranging from carved wooden spoons and combs to hand-knit items such as authentic Rhodope wool blankets.

This is one of the places where the most beautiful yet functional pottery I had ever seen was for sale. I regret not purchasing an entire collection because I have since become obsessed with it. The colors reminded me of Fiestaware brand dishes but with more durability and craftsmanship. It can be described as a colorfully glazed workmanship. The pottery is a craft dating back thousands of years influenced by at least four civilizations passed down from generation to generation.

Not only are the pottery colors and designs perfected but the recipes that go along with them are tried and true. A perfect example of this is called *gyuveche*, a pottery created for the Bulgarian cuisine. We ate lunch at the restaurant on the grounds of the monastery and we were very satisfied with the beautiful Bulgarian salads and meats. Momchil's pizza and ribbon sliced cucumbers were the most beautifully displayed and delicious of all the entrees.

Each family of craftsmen have their own pattern and recipes. My father's love of cooking and traditions were passed down to the younger generation. In fact, the soup my niece served in the *gyuveche* bowls with matching lids was the same recipe dad cooked for me a long time ago in Buffalo. Except, we never owned any Bulgarian pottery in our home.

Our journey continued on the same route travelled by my father and Alexi escaping the Communists decades earlier under much different circumstances. This is primarily why we traveled the chosen route in the first place. Were there other sites to see in Bulgaria that were more famous or touristy such as Stara Zagora, the Eyes of God, Nessebar or Sunny Beach? Indeed, but those places could wait because we were on a mission. Unlike the days that my dad came through these roads, we were safe in cars and taking our time to reach the next destination. We were not in a hurry.

Pamporovo

After visiting Asenovgrad, we drove into the mountains to a ski resort where we spent two nights in Pamporovo at the Green Life Family Apartments. After checking into the hotel, we all gathered in the lobby near a fireplace and enjoyed each other's company with what else but...coffee! We were all accommodated in the same building but different floors, one above the other.

Ski season had ended and tourism was relaxingly slow. Even though it was the month of May, the change in elevation could be felt requiring us to wear winter jackets. We took in the crisp clean air and vistas from the balcony of our apartment overlooking its red roofs. I was impressed that there was a kitchenette with a tea kettle and real dishes. This resort reminded me of a ski resort a few hours from my home in New York called Ellicott Valley. I slept well at the resort with its fresh air and I adored the patio overlooking the forest. From here we could see the television tower in the distance. It felt like a real chalet.

Once again, with stroller in tow, Boyko met the family in Pamporovo at the Green Life Family Resort in the Rhodope mountains after they enjoyed lunch with us at the monastery. Rositsa's hotel suite was one floor above ours and I recognized the pitter-patter of an energetic young boy's feet. They were my great-great-nephew, Valentin's. I imagine that he and his brother must remind their grandmother, of her own children; Boyko and Simeon when they were boys themselves.

On one of evenings, we all gathered in Rositsa's suite for drinks and appetizers such as *snezhanka* (similar to Greek tzatziki), hummus, *baba ganoush*, and dried meat called *lukanka*. Her room was the largest, because they were travelling with my great-niece, Tatiana, and they needed more space. Complete with a roaring gas fireplace, a sofa and dining area, these were the type of memories I loved most. We hung out enjoying each other's company without hurrying home. Being gathered together with family is what I remember most. It seemed that every night was an exuberant celebration of life and ended just before midnight.

Both the accommodations and the restaurant meals at the Green Life Family Apartments were hearty. At the ground floor café, the traditional Bulgarian salad was huge and the cheese was plentiful. The green peppers in this salad reminded me of my dad's sweet homegrown peppers. I enjoyed the breakfasts of salami, ham, Bulgarian cheeses served with cucumbers, tomatoes and a variety of jams and butters.

The host who served us was a caring and generous man. While on my search for bottled water one of the days, he assisted me and inquired where I was from. After explaining that I was from Buffalo, a city near Niagara Falls, I told him that I only knew the polite words in Bulgarian and even those were few but that I did know the alphabet. He seemed happy that I was trying to learn and encouraged me that everyone has to start somewhere.

During check-out, Rositsa talked with the manager and discovered that they also own a resort on the Black Sea. Before we left, we discussed the possibility of vacationing there on our next trip. I was assured we wouldn't need to travel through so many mountains.

TV Tower in Snezhanka Peak

Before leaving the mountains to tour further southwest in Bulgaria, we drove to a television tower overlooking the ski slopes where the wind speed was phenomenal in Snezhanka Peak. Thankfully, we took an elevator to the observation deck where it was so windy that it was difficult to walk around its circumference. I remember laughing because we looked so silly trying to stand upright while taking photos. It was difficult to hold onto our camera phones.

On a clear day, we would have been able to see far into the direction of the refugee camp where dad resided in Greece. Maybe we could have seen as far as the Mediterranean Sea. Even in the dense fog, we could see the routes to the neighboring Bulgarian towns below before roaming our way to the next stop. Bulgaria with its beautiful topography and big-hearted, selfless people was the perfect place for a holiday. They have it all: modern conveniences, old world charm, ski resorts, mineral spas, and excellent food.

Every so often we came across half-finished resort projects. It appears that the builders must have run out of money before they were completed. They looked like skeletons laying vacant rusting away. It was sad to see such deserted places in a land where there is so much potential but, today corruption still exists. As our car passed by, I wished the building projects could be saved. The mountains contain beautiful recreational resorts dotted with ski slopes meandering through tall evergreen trees perfect for ecotourism. The day we visited the television tower, the greenish blue evergreen trees emitted an unusual grey eerie feeling. If the trees had a personality of their own, they seemed to emanate the mood my dad must have felt abandoning his family. How people escaped Communism travelling through such a rugged territory only God knows.

Smolyan

Before our dinner reservation at the traditional Bulgarian restaurant, we toured the only modern church I would see built in the current century. In this town, there are many mosques. The Church of Vissarion was the first Orthodox church built in over 130 years, a miracle in light of the region's Turkish past. Boyko again met us along with his young family of four at this church. His in-laws live in one of the nearby small towns which made it more convenient for them to travel overnight with the youngsters. Tatiana was always willing to hold my great-great-nephew, Angel, to distract him for his doting mom.

At this church, Boyko purchased candles for us to light in memorial of my dad. He tried to explain the significance of the burning candles from the perspective of his Christian Orthodox faith in Bulgarian. Not many words are required as the technique is better learned by doing. This was something he may have learned as a boy, a ritual displayed by his mother and grandmother, women of faith. The sparkle in his eyes did the talking. He missed his great-grandfather as much as I missed my dad. The love he had for my father spilled over to me and I could not help but feel the warmth. Our group was photographed on the steps of this church. It became one of my favorite portraits because I loved this town and I was proud of what it stood for. What a joy it was to see the interest my family had in joining us on such a wonderful adventure.

We ate a late afternoon meal in a Bulgarian restaurant called Bulgarche in Smolyan and enjoyed the music of a young female bagpipe musician at her first public solo concert. Dressed in her traditional costume including a bold red and yellow plaid apron, she sounded great. On one side of me sat Gergana and Momchil and the other my husband and Aleksander. Rositsa shared her local fresh river fish with me. My husband ordered a barbequed chicken and Elena had large skewers full of meat. Boyko shared the most refreshing lemonade. We all spoke with our eyes while filling our stomachs. Rositsa danced the *horo* with Valentin. How I cherished those hours.

Shiroka Laka

The next day after checking out of the mountain ski resort, we drove to Shiroka Laka, a quaint town where a school of music for bagpipe players and traditional dancers is located. We would have loved to see the school but unfortunately the day we were in town, the school was not in session. I wondered if the musician we enjoyed listening to the day before attended this school. That didn't stop us from enjoying the quaintness of this place and here we sat outside and enjoyed coffee while the guys bought a deck of cards and played a few hands while we contemplated a visit to a museum.

After leaving Shiroka Laka, we visited a site that was not on our itinerary. I don't remember reading it when I had Rositsa's itinerary translated by Olga into English. It may have been added at the last minute. I was very careful about our actual destinations matching the itinerary. We left it with our adult children back home who may have needed it to find us. That was my fear as irrational as it was.

We were Americans in a far land, anything could happen. We were on roads that had I been driving, would have been difficult navigating with many fallen rocks, sharp inclines and switchbacks some without guardrails. No wonder so many Bulgarian immigrants who come to my country become long distance truck drivers, they are very skilled drivers. It was to the point that I had to close my eyes and pray to remain calm. Not knowing what to expect after that drive in the mountains, I debated whether or not I wanted to visit the cave in Yagodina.

Pearls in a Cave at Yagodina

There were tour guides at the entrance of the park who were selling tickets to go on a jeep tour up into the cliff where it overlooks the most amazing view. I was opposed to going in a jeep after that drive. I could tell that Momchil really wanted to go on the tour but he was kind to me and told them he'd come another time. Near the parking area of the Yagodina Cave, there was a trickling stream with a dry rocky bed. There was a zipline running above it that ended next to an old arched stone bridge probably thousands of years old. Gergana, Tatiana and Rositsa all did the zipline. I was too much of a chicken but to my defense I was nursing a shoulder injury and I didn't need anything to stir it up. Before the tour of the cave, we found an outside café where we all sat enjoying beverages such as Devin bottled water, Italian coffee and Bulgarian beer.

This was a tense moment because I had developed an attitude due to the travel stress I was experiencing. I jokingly said when they come to the USA, I would get even with them and take them somewhere equally scary in its own way like busy New York City or the Los Angeles highways. I didn't want to go in the cave because I was anxious and besides, there might be bats inside. I didn't want to disappoint them. We had come this far and they wanted to see the cave. My husband wanted to go so I relented and took the tour anyway.

We were told once inside we could not turn around. We would have to continue all the way through the cave and exit on the other side. We had to watch our footing inside to prevent slipping and falling due to the high humidity. As nervous as I was, I was glad I went because it was beautiful inside. The rock formations called stalagmites reminded me of Howe Caverns in New York where I visited as a child. Displayed inside were the most beautiful pearls that had formed in the dark. My family was likened to these pearls, bright and cheerful while on this adventure even when I was not.

After the cave tour, Gergana, Elena, Aleksander and Momchil drove to another tourist attraction called Devil's Bridge. I refused to go because I didn't need to go anywhere in a foreign land with the word "devil" in it. I draw the line somewhere so I did miss out. That was fine with me because I had enough excitement for one day.

I recently read that scientists think that Devil's Bridge could be 7000 years old and has quite a mythological story surrounding it. Months later, while reminiscing about the trip, I watched a Facebook video and I regretted not seeing it in person when I could have. Just like the boat ride on the Niagara River, I missed out on a journey I could have had. I understood why my dad returned to the country of his birth. It is a beautiful nation with a surprise around every corner.

Aleksander drove us into the vicinity of the cave but Tatiana drove us out. So, both of them became my heroes that day. Tatiana drove my husband and me as we continued on our journey southwest. Marco and Rositsa lead the way to the next hotel, a spa in Ognyanovo.

On our drive to the hotel knowing I was still carsick, we stopped at a roadside diner which reminded me of an open-air truck stop. I didn't know at the time but this roadside stop was actually planned and on our itinerary. It was an outdoor café overlooking the hills of the region called Pirinsko but my itinerary indicated Yagodovsko hanche which seemed desolate in the middle of nowhere. We stopped and ordered a bowl of *Bob chorba* bean soup as we talked to the owner. In my opinion, he served the best bean soup. We also befriended a husky with beautiful blue eyes. Was it a Siberian husky? The husky at this stop reminded me of my dad's own husky in the United States of America.

Something about the view from this site was special to me yet I still don't know why. I never forgot the beauty of the brick homes and the craftsmanship of the buildings in the valley overlooking the horizon from this outlook. I wondered if the restaurant owner with his dog lived in one of these houses overlooking the beautiful vista.

It was here that I realized Rositsa's finger had been bleeding so she wrapped a leaf around it because we didn't have any bandages. I never found out if she cut her finger on the children's swings or on the zipline at the cave. My husband thinks it was the zipline. Relaxing at the roadside diner petting the dog as Rositsa had a cigarette calmed both of us down. After the rest stop, I jumped into the backseat of Tatiana's car. My husband sat in the passenger seat ready to finish the remainder of the trip to the next hotel. Once again, I sat with my eyes closed mouthing some prayer hoping the ride would end soon.

Abundant Mineral Spas in Ognyanovo

Arriving at the hotel in Ognyanovo was a little slice of heaven. This destination became a hub for us to day trip for the next three days. As soon as we walked through the glass doors into the modern and clean lobby, we knew we were in for a treat. Our family booked four rooms for three nights on the same side of the building. I was shocked as I walked into the bathroom in that it had an American sized bathtub. Rositsa saw the joy on my face and she knew instantly that she had made a great choice at this resort. I couldn't wait to soak my body in the healing mineral waters that always ran hot.

Each room had its own balcony and was furnished with two chairs, a bistro table, and a clothing drying rack. It was decorated with cream colored annuals overlooking the grassy mountains. Our room, along with Rosita's, had its own private entrance where we were next to each other, like a family suite. We could all talk to each other from the patio while still in our spa robes. It was here in Ognyanovo that I admired the owners of the resort who I believe were Greek for their diligence in running such a beautiful place. The furniture was modern and tastefully decorated. It was a quaint boutique hotel with a very relaxing atmosphere that could rival places I've stayed at in my own country.

On Friday, which was day six of our trip, we planned to drive to Bansko to tour the beautiful church in the city center. Realizing we were exhausted, Rositsa reconsidered our itinerary. We started the day with a delightful Bulgarian breakfast then explored the resort neighborhood on foot. I experienced so many roses here. Every color imaginable grew in various gardens: yellow, orange, fuchsia and red. We stopped to smell the roses and they were intoxicating. Elena explained to me that the striped fuchsia rose was the most fragrant and is the variety used for export as a key ingredient in the most exquisite perfumes of the world. Later, we saw on television that the roses were being harvested in the Valley of the Thracian Kings that same week. This was done in the cool early mornings before the sun rose too high

It was here that I saw my first Russian automobile. It looked so old and outdated to me but it was fascinating, something I would never see in the United States of America. It was small, cute and painted artichoke green. I admired it as we walked along a canal to a park where we enjoyed hazelnut chocolate and berry layer cakes with coffee. Cake, roses, coffee and an adorable family all before noon, I indeed was in heaven.

We spent all day enjoying the Ognyanovo Spa Hotel with its mineral pool. To prepare the chef in advance, each afternoon we chose our dinner entrée from a delicious selection. I remember eating chef creations such as pasta Bolognese, chicken skewers, and both Greek and Bulgarian style salads. Although I did not take advantage of the spa massage services, because of my shoulder injury, my family said their prices were affordable and the quality was excellent. Each night we spent long meals together talking about everything from dad's escape to the family's medical history. This was when Rositsa told me that the man I found on Ancestry.com® who went to Cuba was not a relative that she knew of.

On the second night in Ognyanovo, I woke up frightened and in a panic. I wasn't sure what hit me but maybe it was the realization of how far from home I really was. Anyway, I was scared and it made no sense because we were all safe in our rooms adjacent to each other. I chose not to wake anyone up and prayed to God for peace. I started reading my e-mail to see what was going on at home. It was then that I came across an inspirational message from a friend. The timely message was about overcoming fear. That word came at the right time so I prayed as it is written in the scripture:

For God has not given us a spirit of fear, but of power and of love and of a sound mind (2 Tim 1:7).

After I opened the patio door allowing the fresh air from the valley below to flow in, I fell back asleep. The next morning, I messaged Olga to tell her what happened. She understood my fears and tried to console me from Pleven. She was several hours north of me so it wasn't like we could just meet for coffee. She explained that the reason why we were on so many excursions was because my family wanted to show so much of their beloved country to me. When my husband woke up, I told him that I was afraid of travelling through such rugged territory.

The Black Roads of Pirin

At breakfast, I told Momchil that I was homesick because I didn't know how to explain it to him. I hesitated to go on the two scheduled day trips for it meant driving through more of the mountainous routes. We had been in the Rhodope mountain range but that day we were headed into a different range. To make matters worse, I remembered Gergana saying that the Pirin mountain roads where we were headed after breakfast were considered the "black roads." I thought to myself, you mean the routes get scarier? My husband convinced me that we had to continue on to both Leshten and Kovachevitsa with the rest of our party so as not to disappoint them. I don't know how dad and Alexi made it through these roads, I could barely make it in a Mercedes Benz.

Kovachevitsa

A week after we left Buffalo, we found ourselves on a road trip to Kovachevitsa which was well worth the drive through the black roads of the Pirin Mountains. Once on the road, I realized they weren't as black and scary as I had imagined. The roads themselves are actually in better shape than our roads in New York. The plan was to drive to the furthest destination then work our way back towards the spa hotel and enjoy lunch in Leshten.

As we drove through the Pirins, we saw regions where they were timbering wood and stone for construction. These were the flat stones used for roof tiles of the homes in the region. These were the same types of stones used in the 1800's in Kovachevitsa. It was as if the building methods hadn't changed in 100 years in this part of the world. Such homes flourished during the Bulgarian revival period. One only needs to visit such quaint villages to see the designs of stone masons and carpenters. For sure they are the master craftsmen in wood and stone. The architecture was of incredible craftsmanship and walking into its buildings was like walking into another era of time.

This was one of Rositsa's favorite places as it was once the home of a famous author whose writings she admired. She had recently stayed on the premises at one of the inns for a conference. This town was constructed in a way that everyone travels on foot and the cars are parked on the outskirts. The current population of the town had to be small because the place was very quiet.

Interestingly enough, there was a film crew with what appeared to be a Dutch name printed on the side of their white vans. They were the only vehicles driving into the small village on location filming a movie so we had to be completely silent as we passed by some of the buildings. I learned over a year later from Gergana that the movie was produced and I watched the trailer titled "Live Chimneys." Other than the film production company and a handful of other tourists from the United Kingdom along with their short-legged Dachshund wiener dog, the village was peacefully and eerily quiet. I had a strange feeling that I would return to this town some day in the future.

My favorite picture of Gergana and Momchil was taken in this unusually rustic village as they sat together on a stone bench. Dressed in blue and yellow, matching the flower in Gergana's hair, how I appreciated this young photogenic pair. I remember the men would gather together staring at the structures and I wondered often what they discussed. Two civil engineers, one builder and my great-nephew who acted as the interpreter and photographer joined in on the conversations. This happened often on the trip and it was so endearing to see them bond together.

Leshten

After purchasing gifts in the town store where our souvenir books were stamped, we headed back on the road to Leshten. It was lunchtime and we ate traditional Bulgarian cuisine at the local restaurant on their patio overlooking the heavily wooded region. Although partially outdoors, the patio was cozy and the staff was very attentive. Bright dishes of orange shredded carrots and burgundy kidney bean salad along with a vinaigrette cabbage slaw were fresh and delightful. Scrumptious bread and hummus were plentiful along with *rakiya*.

Leshten with its laid-back atmosphere was the type of place where the cats and dogs roamed free. A Bulgarian Shepherd with his black and white head resembling a St. Bernard but with a completely white double-coated fur body lazily laid in the middle of the road with no fear of vehicles. We had to drive around him. I later learned that this type of dog is a working dog important to the herding of sheep and livestock. My dad wasn't the only one targeted by the Communists, this breed of ancient dog was almost obliterated by them who considered its use in farming to be obsolete. In later years, thanks to a few breeders, its population has been steadily growing. It is evident that times have changed because that Bulgarian Shepherd guarding the entrance of town owned it, and he knew it!

On the way back from Leshten to Ognyanovo, we stumbled upon an archeological find from the time of Alexander the Great where we received a tour in English. We learned how the hot springs were vital to the establishment of the settlement thousands of years ago and remains the draw of the region today at the spa resorts. It can be said "as some things change, some things remain the same."

While here, Marco picked up a bow and arrow and found some enjoyment with it. Rositsa and he left before the tour ended to rest at the hotel. While on the tour my husband needed juice for strength and the heat of the day was getting to us all. It always felt good to arrive back at the Ognyanovo Spa Hotel.

Golyam Beglik

On Sunday, a full week after arriving in Sofia, we packed up and left the spa hotel in Ognyanovo. It was no surprise that when we checked out of our room on Sunday, my family had already paid our hotel and restaurant bills. How do you repay such generosity? As for the time I spent at the spa, I could only dream of living in the perfect place for growing my own roses and bathing in the mineral water that flowed so freely.

We headed back to Plovdiv by way of a different route as if we were completing a large circle, a circle of life. Thankfully, this route was a smoother ride. Aleksander did a great job transporting us safely to our next destination, a beautiful lake with an interesting island in the middle called Golyam Beglik. I saw the dam from a distance and it looked quite impressive. Momchil told me this was one of his favorite places because of the beautiful dense treed island contained within. While walking to a lookout area, we admired a sanctuary for peacocks both pure white and turquoise. Armed with his camera hung on a strap around his neck for most of our trip, Momchil along with Gergana were the first of our group to make it down to the waters' edge to catch a glimpse of the reservoir's beauty.

We stayed to eat at a restaurant that sat on a hill above the water's edge. We insisted on paying for our group's lunch and it took much negotiating with the family to allow this considering they were unhappy with some detail of the meal. As all the discussions were being done in Bulgarian, it was then that we realized that we were out of our league here and learned that Bulgarians take food very seriously. I remember Elena ordered a tripe soup and I enjoyed a delicious fish chowder. After the family allowed my husband to pay for the restaurant check, we were happy to continue on to Plovdiv to get a glimpse of the famous cultural city on our way back to the family's village.

2019 European Capital of Culture - Plovdiv

After our journey over the mountains and through the valleys, we stopped in the city of Philippopolis, my family's city. Up to this point, we were saving the tours of the 2019 European Capital of Culture - Plovdiv for the second half of our two-week trip. Like Rome, Philippopolis, now known as Plovdiv, is the only other place in the world that sits on seven hills and contains its own Roman amphitheater. I could never give the city the justice it deserves because there is so much to see there.

Rositsa works in the city and was proud to show us around, even passing the library she worked at for years. To live and work in such a cosmopolitan place is a true blessing. The family's plan was to introduce us to Plovdiv for only a few hours as not to overwhelm us before ending our week-long trip. We would spend another full day or two in the city before the end of our journey. After entering the city from the highway, we struggled to find parking for the cars due to an art festival that was being held called Kapana Fest that weekend.

Some of my favorite memories of Bulgaria were in the City of Plovdiv that day. We passed the library, a modern large aqua pool of fountains, the colorful t-o-g-e-t-h-e-r sign in the city center, the Roman Stadium of Philippopolis and the beautiful Dzhumaya Mosque before stopping to enjoy coffee at a quaint café containing artwork. We sat outside acting very *aylyak, mayna* which means relaxed and worry-free. Here we sat without a care in the world while the colorful flags above our heads were flapping in the warm afternoon breeze.

It was after drinking our coffee that we realized Tatiana's car was towed by the parking enforcements due to a problem with the parking signage. This caused a bit of angst for Marco and Tatiana as they had to locate the car and pay a hefty fine to get it out of the impound on a Sunday. Tatiana's car contained our luggage with items we could not immediately replace, if required. The rest of us piled into the remaining two cars and once back in the village, everything was calm. They don't let anything wreck their jovial social nature. The car was returned and we spent the next three nights in my niece's home, the old homestead of my father.

Chapter 16. Home Away from Home

On the way back to Rositsa's home, we again stopped at my brother-in-law's home where we found the last two jars of the *lutenitza*, a famous Bulgarian red pepper condiment preserved the previous harvest season. The peppers are roasted and cooked with tomatoes and other ingredients for almost a day. Over an outdoor fire in a black cast iron cauldron, it had become a thick and chunky bright red reduction. He gladly gave the sealed jars to us to enjoy with the evening's meal. Later that afternoon, at home in the village, there was a rainbow overlooking Rositsa's yard. We took this as a good sign of God's promises.

We continued on with another long meal including the bean soup, *Bob chorba*, served in the *gyuveche* clay pots with their glazed lids, cooked by Ekaterina. She had stayed behind with my great-nephew, Sergey, while we traveled the previous week. He and his grandmother took care of the house and fed the animals while we were away. Along with the salad, we opened a jar of the preserved condiment and spread it on the freshest baked white bread topped with feta cheese and a dry spice called *chubritsa*, a form of savory. For dessert we ate wonderful Turkish pastries that Rositsa stopped to purchase at a specialty bakery on our way home from the mineral spa. It was an end to a perfect first holiday week with my family except that one of the twin kittens was missing. He escaped possibly through the infamous front gate while we were on holiday and Sergey was on a mission to find him.

For the remainder of the trip, Rositsa and her husband roomed with Tatiana while my husband and I took over the master suite which was very private across the hall from Sergey. Tatiana's caged bird got loose and we were told using hand gestures to watch for it because it may have made it to the second floor trying to get out through the open windows. From the second story window, I had a bird's eye view of the land dad once owned.

Agriturismo

On day nine of our Bulgarian trip, the beginning of a new week, we spent a quiet day at Rositsa's home cooking while Marco mowed the lawn. Tatiana made a plain New York style cheesecake filled in a graham cracker crust with the most delicious wild strawberry preserves. These strawberries were the size of plump rehydrated raisins, little and sweet. She had purchased the preserved strawberries in one of the little towns at a roadside stand while on our journey the previous week. I hadn't even considered buying such delicacies knowing it would be impossible to get them through our airport customs. It was coincidental that strawberries were such a hit on this trip when it was the strawberry that was dad's largest export prior to the regime's takeover.

Although tomatoes were not in season yet, my niece had purchased the largest, ripest tomatoes from the market resembling the tomatoes I've tasted from New Jersey. I noticed that the produce in Bulgaria was different than ours at home. It tasted more real and less commercial. It made me think of my father's homeland as an *agriturismo*, a concept I learned about in Italy. Rivalling Italy, the food and the hospitality is something the Bulgarians ought to be proud of. With my family, I was invited to my very own *agriturismo*. Rositsa cooked fresh eggs each morning from the hens in her barn. I even learned how to make *tarator*, a traditional cucumber and yogurt chilled soup, the same recipe my family prepared for the workers in the orchards before Bulgaria had changed and dad left.

I learned from Ivan that during the Cold War while dad was in the United States of America, my brother's tomatoes ripened on his land before the state-run working farms. Although it infuriated the BCP, this was something that made dad proud of his only son. My family's "green thumb" had been passed down from generation to generation.

In the gardens we found snails in beautiful shells reminding me of the ocean, something I never expected to see in the backyard. For all I knew they could be a pest or a nuisance but I thought they were beautiful. It was laundry day and my niece laundered some of the clothes we still needed for the second half of our trip. The grapes that grew over the arbor constructed of pipes covered the yard and doubled as a laundry rack.

In the kitchen, my niece made moussaka with potatoes, beef and a Béchamel sauce for the topping. As we lingered in the yard lazily with the three yellow cats with Italian names such as Limoncello and Arancini, we admired the workmanship of the solar panels that heated the water for our hot showers. The cats slept near the solar panels warming themselves in the sun of the day. It was during this afternoon that something truly special occurred but I only realized it in hindsight, so I will explain later.

The Joy of the Dance

My sister, Blagorodna, 25 years older than me, took me by surprise. Although a generation older, she seemed modern and hip. For one reason, I felt sheer joy when her family taught me Bulgarian folk dancing. Body language became important due to the fact that we could not understand each other without our translators. Yet the bond we felt spoke volumes. Bulgarians have a traditional culture with a distinct religion, ceremonies, holidays and amazing folk dances with costumes.

Blagorodna's two-year-old great-grandson, Tosho, gave me a beautiful pink flower the afternoon we were invited to her home for dinner. It was late afternoon and the lace floor to ceiling curtains were drawn. Together in the privacy of her immaculate home we had a lavish meal and conversations that needed to be had for a long time. Ten of us including Tosho gathered in my sister's dining room over homegrown potatoes and free-range chicken adjacent to a living room and television.

We enjoyed the *shopska salad* that was so fresh and arranged with perfection topped with carefully arranged parsley. They served a traditional homemade dried pork meat carefully sliced and arranged in a round pattern on a serving plate. The meal was complete with the most delicious dessert that reminded me of a chocolate ganache cake along with mouth-watering assorted cookies. The evening would not be complete without their homemade *rakiya* and a strong homemade red wine for me. They also had a special *rakiya* made with bee pollen. It was the best.

It was here among the photos that I found one of my favorite family portraits from the 1980's. My dad was with his wife and all the children and grandchildren on the porch of one of the homes. I couldn't tell which home it was but I could recognize almost every face in the picture. They shared all the photos that they had of my dad with me that night. My sister was content to listen with patience as her grandson did all of the interpreting.

I learned that my sister loved to sew. Upon meeting a week earlier, I had presented her with a French cream damask print apron lined with a yellow bee print that I had sewn for her to use in the garden. It seemed that the talent for sewing was generational as my sisters, including the late Tanya, all had a knack for it. The bee printed fabric seemed to foreshadow the delicious bee products they gave us to take home.

Remember when I explained that I suspected my dad died in the village in which he lived? Well it was Blagorodna, who told me that dad died from a stroke while riding his bicycle to a neighboring village to get a haircut. In his possession was a thermos of coffee and a box of chocolates. Prior to this evening I hadn't learned of my father's cause of death and this brought me some closure.

Stoyko, a devoted father and husband, was so tender-hearted and modest with his English, apologizing as he went along. An engineer, I was quite impressed with his skills and could only imagine how proud my dad would be of all his great-grandsons. Each of them is gentle in nature, just like him. As was dad, Stoyko is very protective of his family. They sent us home with honey collected from their own property in a beautiful jar which endured the flight home along with artwork and a handwoven tapestry. They were as sweet and joyful as the honey I savored. I only hope that this book encourages Blagorodna to write about her own experiences with dad for her great-grandchildren.

Restored Ancient Basilica

We started our tour of Plovdiv at a small restored basilica dating back to the year 471 A.D. What struck me the most at this site was its cross-shaped baptismal. The mosaics were designed with several materials but the detail in the pictures of the mosaics were symbolic to our faith as Christians. There were doves representing the Holy Spirit, rosettes signifying the blood of Jesus, and the Solomon's knot symbolizing eternity. I had never seen anything like it before. All of these antiquities are housed in a burnt orange colored modern building, indicative of a mix of civilizations, old and new.

Thrilled in the Theater

Finally, after months of admiring pictures of the Roman Theater of Plovdiv, on day ten we were finally on our way to see the ancient landmark I had only dreamed of seeing in person. The Roman Theater is different from the Roman Stadium we had seen two days earlier. Tanya's grandson, Radoslav, accompanied us on the remainder of our trip as his exams had ended. It was a joyous day because for the first time we had Radoslav and Sergey together at the same time and the family gathering together grew. We walked over a real Roman road, possibly the same path the apostle Paul may have walked on his way to Macedonia. We stopped at several destinations in the city learning about its amazing history and culture.

Never had I been in a more rugged city where we stepped over so many different types of stones and eras of architecture. Flowers bloomed everywhere including wild red roses growing on the iron gates protecting the Roman Theatre. The grandeur of the place is unmistakable. I was sad that my dad never got to enjoy such a marvelous place as the archeological site wasn't uncovered until after he died. We were there admiring it for him. Views from the city are all picturesque. The cantilevered Bulgarian Revival homes were painted in vibrant colors of orange, blue, green and yellow. The striking black wrought ironwork and clay roof tiles are everywhere. The ethnographic museum, one of the most ornate buildings, was a hit with not only us foreigners but the seasoned Bulgarians learned about the same ancestors we were equally a part of. We all learned something.

The shopping district called The Trap with its high-end luxury brands reminded me a bit of Copenhagen and it is lovely. If I were to describe Plovdiv, I would say it is full of color and texture. As Momchil stood at the foot of a hill, he photographed our group in the background of shrubs manicured into the word 'Plovdiv' in the Cyrillic alphabet. Unknown to Plovdiv itself, the city brought us together in 2017 to a real European Capital of Culture two years prior to its official unveiling.

Warm Hospitality

On our way back to Rositsa's, we were invited to the home of Violeta for an afternoon treat of snacks, beverages and conversation in a decorated building reminding me of a beautiful cabana. Here we met her family including her son, Rumen; oldest granddaughter, Nedelya; and her husband. I had met Nedelya's sister, Emilia, a week earlier. Nedelya had dance lessons that afternoon so she was dressed in her traditional costume. It was exciting to meet my niece's husband and talk to him. He told us the story that his own grandfather had served time in Belene and that dad's stay there was about a year and a half. Each day with these people was exciting for different reasons.

Celebrating Two Saints and the Alphabet

Then on day 11, the celebration of Saints Cyril and Methodius arrived and it rained. Most of the day we spent quietly relaxing at home with Rositsa and her family enjoying each other's company along with the kittens. The playful chocolate kitten that had been lost the week we were on vacation had been found. As my great-nephew, Sergey, drove through the village he found his sweet kitten running on one of the roads. He was happily reunited with the other cats. Many days we played with the kittens which never required the right language, it was a universal language.

Since it was a national holiday, it was a great occasion to make a traditional meal of roasted chicken in pickled cabbage with rice. In the kitchen again with Rositsa, she showed me how to make the recipe. We lined the roasting pan with cabbage leaves. The preserved cabbage with water and salt was drained and placed on top of the cabbage leaves. Then we layered the chicken and partially cooked rice on top. Lastly, we added another layer of fresh cabbage then baked it. It made for the most tender chicken. They were from her own barn in that they were slaughtered, plucked and frozen months earlier. I remember Rositsa telling me how she hated this job but her mother insisted they were the tastiest chickens available.

Let Sleeping Cats Lie

This holiday was memorable to me not only because it was Rositsa's favorite holiday but because I was able to meet my great-nephew, Simeon, and my niece, Boyana, for the first time. Boyana was the granddaughter who played with the ball near the barn so my dad could watch her from a distance while he hid decades earlier. They celebrated the day with us by arriving with my oldest sister, Anelia, so I could visit with her one more time before I departed the village the next day. They arrived with so many gifts and a delicious Bulgarian cake with cream and nuts.

On this particular day, Radoslav translated for us. A humorous thing happened when Anelia sat next to me. The two kittens were already asleep next to me on the banquette against the windows but she could not see them from where she stood. I carefully scooped up the kittens in my hands and moved them between Radoslav and myself as they remained asleep at the corner of the cushioned benches. I did this so that she would not sit on them by mistake. This upset my sister as she thought I should have let them be. I didn't understand her but Radoslav translated for me.

"You can tell the character of a person by how they treat animals," Radoslav said. I asked him to tell her in Bulgarian that I actually love animals. The saying "let sleeping dogs lie" must also refer to cats in Bulgaria. It made for an awkward moment but it was quite funny. Radoslav advised me not to move the kittens again. The moral of the story is in Bulgaria, "let sleeping cats lie."

I sat on Anelia's left side with our backs to the windows while my great-nephews sat across from us. I imagine in looking at us, they could see the resemblance in our jawlines, noses and skin tone even if we were 35 years apart in age. Boyko's younger brother, Simeon, had an amazing smile and his tee-shirt read, "Another State of Mind." It described my feelings about being in another state of mind. I was in disbelief that after so many years, I finally met the boys I read about 29 years earlier in my family's letter. This is when I learned that Anelia and dad had sent more letters but they must have either been lost or confiscated by the Communists because I never received them. We said our farewells and I was sad to see them leave.

Joy of the Dance

Before my trip, I wrote a letter to my mom's oldest sister who lives in the State of Arizona asking her to tell me what she remembered about my childhood with my dad. I wanted to share her information with my nieces and nephews while in Bulgaria. In her reply letter, she mentioned that he danced and sang to me in Bulgarian. She wrote how he was very protective and gave me all his love like any good father would.

Dance can be many things; an expression of oneself, as part of worship to God, exercise for the mind, body and soul or an outlet for pleasure. Later that evening, I was again invited to the home of my sister, Blagorodna. They served us beverages and snacks since we had already eaten dinner at Rositsa's. This was when I joyfully danced the *horo* for the first time without feeling self-conscious.

Dance can also break down walls. When the Berlin wall fell, didn't we dance in the streets across the world as we celebrated? Although I was introduced to the *horo* at picnics and birthday parties in Buffalo, I never felt entirely comfortable dancing the *horo* until I met Blagorodna's family. It was with them that I danced freely and whenever I think about the experience, it makes me smile with joy. They were all great dancers. No surprise given that they start young. The dance my father enjoyed with me as a small child reminded me of the joy I felt as I danced with Tosho with his family cheering on as the television broadcasted traditional folk music. I suspect that the tradition that my family kept in folk dancing was passed down to them by my own father. I know he would have been proud of his great-great-grandson's ability. Tosho learned to dance before the age of two and he became my dance partner on my last night in the family's village. This was my last dance in Bulgaria.

Chapter 17. Culture Through Flowers

I n Bulgaria, like many places around the world, poppies grow in the wild. They reminded me that God shows Himself through nature as it is written in the scripture:

Let the fields be jubilant, and everything in them; let all the trees of the forest sing for joy (Ps 96:12).

These vibrant reddish-orange flowers were blooming the month we arrived. We too have flowers just as beautiful as Bulgarian poppies. It was through these quirky flowers though that I was able to better understand the culture. I saw the kindness of a nation. The generosity I experienced was multi-faceted. Their kindness was shown through both subtle and non-subtle ways. One of the subtle ways was through the gift of flowers. As we journeyed on our predetermined route, we always enjoyed the outdoors. Anyone who has travelled through this land understands its unmistakable beauty.

While touring picturesque mountains, driving through rolling hills and wandering over a Roman road, we stopped to enjoy the flowers. Whether admiring fields full of poppies, smelling delicious fragrant roses that peeked through fences to reach for the sun, or stretching our own heads up to see the beginning of the bloom of a magnolia tree, stopped we did! One after the other, the women picked certain flowers and presented them to me.

It all started at the airport upon my arrival. My family greeted me with a white basket of arranged flowers from my niece's own garden. As we left on our family vacation departing my niece's home, my elderly sister-in-law picked a few leaves from a plant that is traditionally given as a gift for a journey. This was the day we visited the old monastery. As we drove to our destination, I knew the chance of this greenery surviving the day was slim. She had given this carefully-wrapped foliage for good reason and I wanted to be entrusted with it. As it wilted in the back seat on the rubber floor mat of my nephew's car, I was determined that before it was fully limp, I would capture a photo of it. At least the photo would survive our trip.

Then after touring the ski resort while walking to tour one of the nearby towns, Elena showed me a poppy still nestled in its pod. After removing the outside layer, the resulting bud resembled a doll's beautiful orange skirt. How creative I thought for her to envision such a transformation. She gave it to me and I carried it as a souvenir through the town as we went looking for a museum. That evening as we arrived at The Green Life Family Apartments, I placed the poppy in a small glass with the other greenery I had been given. The next morning after I awoke, I surprisingly found that not only did the greenery perk up, the poppy had fully transformed from the skirted pod into a full mature bloom. I saw it as a sign of a great journey ahead of us. It was a symbol of our own family's revival.

During our trip near Greece, Tatiana gave me a tiny bouquet of white flowers with yellow centers resembling daisies she had gathered and carefully tied together with a vine. In the quietness of my hotel room, I unwrapped the vine to photograph the loosened flowers. The curled vine reminded me of the scripture as it is written:

"I am the vine; you are the branches. He who abides in Me, and I in him, bears much fruit; for without Me you can do nothing" (John 15:5).

Towards the end of my stay, Ekaterina gave me a pink flower with a yellow center and well-defined medium green leaves as a farewell gift. It survived the two-hour journey to Sofia and perked up in a glass of water. It was as strong two days later when I left it with Elena the same way I had received it.

Chapter 18. Leaving the Village Behind

Day 12 of our journey was the last morning we were to wake up in Rositsa's home and it was emotional. Like all mornings, she was up early cooking our meals. As a special good-bye, she made fried flattened doughnuts called *mekitsi*, one of her father's favorite treats. Served with honey, we both sensed the loss we would feel knowing we were departing the village that day. Rositsa's family arranged the time for Aleksander to pick us up. He and his family had been staying at his dad's house a short drive away. He would be driving us back to his home in Sofia to spend the two remaining days.

Blagorodna's family were also outside the gate in the street waiting for us as they gave their own farewells. This was the gate guarded by the militia over 50 years earlier. As I turned and looked back, I snapped a picture through the back window of the car to capture the memory. I wondered if it was the same feeling dad had when he left the same family decades earlier. I could see that they were just as grieved as I was. The sadness on their faces brought tears to my eyes.

I was saying goodbye to my own sister not knowing if I'd ever see her again. Every day since I had arrived her two-year old grandson, Tosho, asked his mom about me. Now I had to say good-bye to the small boy. How could he understand why I was leaving? He waved goodbye with the same hand he held up high the night before as we danced the *horo*.

The good-byes got more difficult as the next two days went on. Our next stop was Violeta's home where she and her family were waiting in the courtyard to give their last regards. The same way we clung to each other when we first met, we did again. Violeta and I looked for a translator who could help us in our last few moments together. In the hustle and bustle, only we knew the desperation we felt not being able to communicate at will. We both hung on to each other and the hope that we'd see each other again someday. How I miss my nieces and nephews.

Boyana, The Foothills of Vitosha

On the day we returned to Sofia, five of us toured the church in the Boyana neighborhood of Sofia. Elena stayed behind to unpack from the trip and to prepare the evening's meal. Five of us explored the garden and sat on a stone fence waiting patiently to be admitted through the short door marred by invading tribes hundreds of years earlier. It was one of the only surviving Christian churches in the area during the Ottoman-Turk rule. The small but heavily frescoed walls were very well protected by the tour guides. No photos were allowed in this holy sanctuary. Set into the foothills of the Vitosha Mountain, it was securely gated and surrounded by large sequoia trees.

Honey and Home Cooking

After we returned to Aleksander's home, Momchil opened four different varieties of honey he purchased while we traveled the previous week. We had a honey tasting with a full set of tiny spoons set out by Elena. One at a time, we dipped a spoon into the amber colored jars in four different hues and experienced flavors of honey that I didn't know existed. It was like a flavor explosion that I could not contain myself.

"Oh my God, it's so good!" I gasped.

It was so generous of Momchil to offer such an indulgence. He offered more but I didn't want to eat all his special honey. Any more than that may have given me a stomach ache anyway. That evening, Elena had prepared a traditional recipe of sautéed green peppers, cheese and egg recipe called *mish mash* served with meats, cheeses and bread. We were spoiled by all the great homecooked meals we were served but oh so thankful.

Our last full day in Bulgaria started with a homemade *banitza* baked by Elena and cut into squares including side dishes with a large amount of yogurt. Aleksander brewed my favorite cappuccino after he ran to the store for some strange Bulgarian fermented beverage called *Boza*. I think it was an acquired taste that I could eventually get accustomed to. They anticipated that we would not like it. We felt bad not finishing our glasses. They definitely deserved an "A" for effort in trying to provide us with all the Bulgarian foods to experience. Breakfast was unhurried as we enjoyed it with what seemed like an entire flat of ripe strawberries between seven of us.

Free Sofia Tour

We arranged our time on our final day to go on a "Free Sofia Tour" after breakfast. The tour guide met us outside the Palace of Justice by the lion statue. On my first day in the city as we travelled from the airport, we passed the St. Sofia Statue and I wondered about this imposing building nearby. It was within the square with the former Bulgarian Communist Party building and they were all grand in size. I listened as he had fascinating historical information about Bulgaria all in English. We learned through archaeological discoveries that it is quite possible that Sofia, or Serdica as it was known, could be 8,000 years old versus the previous thought of 6,000 years of continuous habitation.

There were so many eras represented in one city. Old brick churches were attached to newer structures. For quite a while we stood before the St. George Church – the Rotunda where we learned about the Square of Tolerance for religion that Sofia has been known for. All within a few-minute walk, you find the Sofia Synagogue, the Banya Bashi Mosque, the St. Joseph Catholic Church and the Sveta Nedelya Cathedral each representing a different faith proving that all people could live together. We also learned a story about how Tsar Boris III was late for the funeral of a prominent member of society and before he arrived at the Sveta Nedelya Church it had been bombed tragically killing hundreds inside. Thankfully, he was not assassinated and the church has since been rebuilt.

We walked through ancient ruins and the tour guide explained that when they are uncovered, they are topped with a line of red brick indicating a change in civilizations. This was also done in the ruins near the spa we visited the previous week near Ognyanovo but I hadn't fully grasped the concept until this tour.

Architectural arches were built along with monstrous Communist era buildings. The National Theater of Ivan Vazov with its columns and engraved statues was remarkably ornate. We even passed the Russian Church with what looked like three golden crowns. The hot water flowing out of the hot spring fountains are still used today as people fill their water bottles. The tour ended at the grand Aleksander Nevsky Cathedral where our trip had started almost two weeks earlier.

Inspiration for a Cover Photo in Sofia

After the tour, we parked Aleksander's car and walked through a residential neighborhood to a cafe. On the way, I was enamored with the view of an old building abutting a modern building with a red tiled wall. At the time, I didn't know why I was so drawn to it. A few steps ahead of me, Momchil turned around to see what I was photographing this time. I snapped a few photos and went on my way to keep up with the others. The entrance of the restaurant was covered with a beautiful crawling ivy and for over an hour we lingered there. The café reminded me of a rainforest and had a greenhouse vibe retaining the heat of the day. It warmed us as we enjoyed delicious soups in homemade bread bowls.

We continued our journey through fabulous Sofia stopping to talk about the statue of Aleko Konstantinov who wrote the famous work "To Chicago and Back." During our time together, Gergana had told me about this book and encouraged me to read it. I found it to be an interesting coincidence that Aleko travelled to this part of my country. We walked along the famous fountain promenade at the Palace of Culture. At the top of the bridge near the palace there was an art exhibition with each of the Cyrillic alphabet symbols or letters on display where we had a great view of the city street below. We headed back to the car crossing through a large park with a Japanese Garden. We would have stayed longer but we all wanted to get back to the car before the parking meter expired. No one needed another parking fine.

After our tour of Sofia, we took a siesta while the Bulgarians worked and cooked. Prior to my trip to Bulgaria, a few of my friends tried to share tips about their homeland to help prepare for me the culture change. The two biggest differences I found with their culture are the concept of an afternoon siesta and the traditions passed down from generation to generation. In the United States of America, we fail to rest enough or keep traditions alive long enough to pass them down to the next generation. It was difficult to get used to the idea of an afternoon nap and to be polite, I asked how long were we supposed to stay in our room so as not to sleep too long. I was told a minimum of two hours. It was evident that we had exhausted our hosts. I doubt they had time to rest themselves as they had to catch up with work and prepare the evening meal. We were only so happy to oblige in order to have time to ourselves. The tour had tired us out.

The River that Flows Freely

Later, Gergana asked me what I liked the most about the Sofia tour. I needed time to ponder this. It was a tough decision but later when she asked again, I said that I loved the elegance of the bathhouse. Actually, I love the fact that hot water flows freely from the water fountains in the city due to the underground hot springs, one of the reasons Serdica was made popular in ancient times. The water that flowed back then continues to water the land today and is a spiritual symbol of the life that flows through my father's homeland. As it is written in the scripture:

And he showed me a pure river of water of life, clear as crystal, proceeding from the throne of God and of the Lamb. In the middle of its street, and on either side of the river, was the tree of life, which bore twelve fruits, each tree yielding its fruit every month. The leaves of the tree were for the healing of the nations (Rev 22:1-2).

The Last Supper

That last evening, before our departure for New York, Tatiana, Rositsa and one of her very close friends from Sofia joined all of us for dinner. Tatiana and Rositsa had arrived in Sofia on Saturday to stay overnight with their friend so they could meet us at the airport to say goodbye one last time. They arrived at Aleksander's home by taxi. Elena cooked a meal with pork and mushrooms as the main ingredients. She created an exquisite mushroom sauce that was so delicious that we still rave about it today. We said our final farewells to Rositsa's friend along with Momchil and Gergana after dinner. Just like the two weeks we all spent inseparable, that night went too fast.

See You Soon. *Do Skoro*!

Our flight the next morning was early and we were anxious to make it through security not to miss any of the three flights home. We woke up by 4:00 A.M. Five of us along, with our luggage, packed into the car. Aleksander drove us back through Sofia towards the airport in the sad dark quiet hours passing all the places I already mentioned. This time, it was Radoslav's turn to translate. He was so kind to offer to translate for us at the Austrian Airlines' checked baggage counter. We wanted to be sure all of our precious Bulgarian souvenirs made it home safely. We took notice of all these little nuances and we were most impressed by him, Momchil and their entire generation. The family took care of every last detail. They don't even realize they are doing anything significant; it's in their nature. Inside the airport, Rositsa and Tatiana appeared as tired as the rest of us to bid their own farewells.

I kept repeating the phrase "*Do skoro!*" which means to see you soon. I never wanted to say good-bye. Leaving their sides as they stood on the ground floor looking up as our escalator rose taking us further away from each other, was the hardest part. Once through immigration, the realization that I was going home to a different part of the world without them saddened me and as I walked towards our gate, I cried. In less than 24 hours, we arrived back in Buffalo, forever changed.

Epilogue

The Cherry Tree, A Realization

Remember when I said something truly special happened on day nine of our trip? I think now is the right time to share my realization. If I hadn't made it clear earlier, my niece's home was a respite even for the storks as we were in awe of the huge nest overlooking the backyard, part of a 32-acre parcel shared by my four siblings.

When we weren't touring the neighboring city of Plovdiv or the southwestern part of Bulgaria, we were relaxing at her home in the village. One such day, Rositsa let us taste the ripe cherries that were in season. Marco set up a ladder to pick the ripest cherries high up in the tree, while Rositsa told me the story of the tract of land the tree now sits on. As the story goes according to her, my dad and his friend survived their journey through Bulgaria under harsh conditions. As I'd already written, once arriving back into my family's village while under surveillance, the officer found refuge with my great-aunt while my dad hid in the business building in the homestead barn for the winter.

The property looked as if over the years parts of the home had been renovated while other buildings were demolished and removed. The cherry tree that we ate from stood at the very place my dad hid while the entire family faced a death penalty for harboring him. The difference now being that we were free to eat from a tree that doesn't grow in a greenhouse or in a pot. It has no restrictions on it for time was kind to the tree allowing it to grow strong and fruitful. The soil beneath it was replenished by the salt in the tears of my dad's loneliness. As we contemplated the significance of the tree each in our own language, we knew that the love my dad had for us was now feeding us its fruit.

Conclusion

B eing half Bulgarian, I am blessed because I have the best of both worlds. I have been born and raised in the United States of America with all of its benefits, but I also feel a kinship for this ancient land of Bulgaria. I am on the outside looking in. Because of the love of a father, I have much love for the nation of his birth. I did not have to escape the Communists or suffer under socialist programs like others. I did not struggle to raise children in a broken economy like my nieces and nephews. This gives me a perspective to see things that a native Bulgarian may not. I see their potential.

Why some people were afforded the opportunity to live in the United States of America while others remained behind only God knows. My feeling is that we don't live where we live by accident, we live where we do for a reason and that it is all planned by God. This is why it is so important to love and pray for our neighbors.

It is true that many of Bulgaria's people have left for greener pastures. They left for political and economic reasons. The youth have moved to the cities for jobs leaving the older generation behind. They seek education and work opportunities in other European countries and abroad. Even the migrants looking to escape their Middle Eastern countries prefer to pass through Bulgaria to seek asylum in a more prosperous country like Germany, The Netherlands, Belgium or France. The older generation that endured the changes in the government and have much wisdom are passing away. The opportunities in my father's homeland are not as numerous as one would desire although things are slowing improving.

I dream of restoration, redemption and restitution. As in Elijah's day, I see a cloud the size of a man's hand as it is written in the scripture:

Then it came to pass the seventh time, that he said, "There is a cloud, as small as a man's hand, rising out of the sea!" So, he said, "Go up, say to Ahab, 'Prepare your chariot, and go down before the rain stops you'" (1 Kings 18:44).

Most Bulgarians I have met in the USA do not wish to return to Bulgaria because they enjoy the lives they have built here in the United States of America. I am happy for them and glad that they have embraced our culture and add so much to our society. Although they have adjusted to their new lives here, I can tell they miss their old world and it is unspoken. A slower pace with vibrant conversation over endless meals and a sense of community was left behind. As one Bulgarian lady told me, in the USA, she needs to make an appointment a week in advance to meet a friend for coffee. In Bulgaria, they just meet.

There is a special gentleness and selflessness that exists with these people. I see it in both the old and young alike. On occasion, I have met a few native Bulgarians who see the cloud of hope I see; a revival both spiritual and financial. Would some contribute to the rebuilding of the nation after Communism? They didn't leave because they hated the culture, on the contrary, the culture is what everyone misses, including myself. Maybe some Bulgarians will return home. Will they return after being educated abroad to enact the economic models they have studied? Will they renovate the abandoned homes in the villages that their grandparents are leaving behind? Will they retire back home with their Social Security payments? How can we as people who live in the new world possibly forget the old world's cradle of civilization? Has Bulgaria's time arrived?

There is a time for everything under heaven as it is written in the scripture:

To everything there is a season, A Time for every purpose under heaven;

A time to be born, and a time to die;

A time to plant and a time to pluck what is planted;

A time to kill, and a time to heal,

A time to break down, and a time to build up;

A time to weep, and a time to laugh;

A time to mourn, and a time to dance;

A time to cast away stones and a time to gather stones;

A time to embrace and a time to refrain from embracing;

A time to gain and a time to lose;

A time to keep, and a time to throw away;

A time to tear, and a time to sew;

A time to keep silence, and a time to speak;

A time to love, and a time to hate;

A time of war, and a time of peace

(Eccl 3:1-8).

While sharing excerpts of my book with a group of native Bulgarian women prior to publishing, I realized that it made them sad. I wondered if the way in which I told the story was gentle enough. It was then that they told me that the hope I mentioned in the form of a cloud reminded them of a sentimental song in Bulgaria about an immigrant which caused them to miss their motherland. There is a link to the song based on a poem by Ran Bosilek in Appendix D.

I am hopeful that the readers of my book will be encouraged to visit Bulgaria and experience this 2019 European Capital of Culture in Plovdiv and that some people, like my dad, will be brave enough to return home.

PART IV

APPENDICES

Appendix A

The Translated Bulgarian Letter

Date: December 26, 1988

Dear child Lisa,

I am the oldest daughter of [Peter Nikodimov Avramov]. Today is Christmas 26-Dec-1988. For the first time, today, my father showed me your letters and photos that you sent in March of 1988. He had started to write back a few times but he has forgotten English and he gave up. I cried a lot for you dear Lisa. I cried for a child that is looking for her father, same as us, four kids, looked and waited 30 years for our father. When he got back to Bulgaria, he was very happy to find his four children and his wife healthy and alive. My mother died three years ago.

Dear Lisa, my father lived with my brother. We are three sisters and one brother. Dad now lives with me, [Anelia] and my husband [Hristo]. For now, my father's health is very good. He is 78 years old. Now that I asked him why doesn't he write to you at least in Bulgarian he is sending you his best regards and is wishing you to be a healthy and happy child and that he thinks of you just as you think of him, but destiny…

Lisa, my father and I can't wait to hear from you and to tell us how do you live. Put a picture of yourself in the envelope also.

Lisa, you should know that I want to have correspondence with you and how dear you are to me. I have only one daughter, [Boyana], and she has two boys, [Boyko] and [Simeon].

Accept our best wishes from Bulgaria, I wish you all the best. Kisses from your sister [Anelia] and your dad [Peter Nikodimov Avramov].

Wishing you a Merry Christmas and a Happy New Year 1989. Let God's Blessing be always with you and give you health, good luck in your marriage and a lot of success in life.

With respect, [Anelia] and [Peter Nikodimov Avramov]

The names in the [brackets] above reflect the characters in this story. Although the letter is true to its' translation, the names are fictitious.

Appendix B

Names and Relationships of Characters

Name	Relationship
Aleksander	Son of Tanya; Father of Momchil & Radoslav; Nephew of Lisa; Husband of Elena; Brother of Violeta
Alexi	Bulgarian Friend of Peter; Father of Mitko and Stoyan; Husband of Lila
Anastasia	American sister of Lisa
Anelia	Oldest sister of Lisa; Daughter of Peter & Ruska; author of Bulgarian letter
Angel	Son of Boyko; Great-great-nephew of Lisa; Brother of Valentin
Blagorodna	Daughter of Peter & Ruska; Mother of Janeta; Sister of Lisa
Bogdan	American Sponsor to Peter and Ivan
Borislav	Husband of Tanya; Brother-in-law of Lisa
Boyana	Daughter of Anelia; Niece of Lisa; Mother of Boyko & Simeon
Boyko	Son of Boyana; Grandson of Anelia; Great-nephew of Lisa; Father of Valentin & Angel; Great-grandson of Peter
Corinne	Clerk at State University of New York at Buffalo
Dinko	Friend of Vasil
Diyana	Daughter of Simeon; Great-great-niece of Lisa
Ekaterina	Sister-in-law of Lisa; Wife of Vasil; Mother of Rositsa

Elena	Wife of Aleksander; Mother of Momchil & Radoslav; Daughter-in-law of Tanya
Elizabeth	American niece of Lisa
Emil	Husband of Janeta; Father of Stoyko
Emiliya	Daughter of Rumen; Great-great-niece of Lisa
Gabby	Sister of Bogdan Vazov
George	Fieldworker of Peter & Ruska
Gergana	Girlfriend of Momchil
Helga	Mother of Alexi
Hristo	Husband of Anelia; Father of Boyana; Grandfather of Boyko & Simeon; Brother-in-law of Lisa
Ivan	Peter's Bulgarian Friend; Uncle of Maria
Jacob	American son of Lisa
Janeta	Daughter of Blagorodna; Mother of Stoyko; Grandmother of Tosho
Kiro	Adoptive Father of Peter; Husband of Luba
Lila	Wife of Alexi
Lisa	American Daughter of Peter & Natalie; Sister of Anelia, Tanya, Vasil & Blagorodna; Sister of Anastasia; Mother of Jacob
Luba	Wife of Grandpa Kiro
Marco	Husband of Rositsa
Maria	Niece of Ivan
Mariela	Wife of Stoyko; Mother of Tosho; Daughter-in-law of Janeta
Michelle	American niece of Lisa's husband, Tom
Mikhail	Husband of Blagorodna; Father of Janeta; Brother-in-law of Lisa

Mitko	Son of Alexi & Lila; Brother of Stoyan
Momchil	Son of Aleksander; Brother of Radoslav; Great-nephew of Lisa; Grandson of Tanya
Natalie	Mother of Lisa; Long-term American Girlfriend of Peter; Mother of Anastasia
Nedelya	Daughter of Rumen; Granddaughter of Violeta; Great-great-niece of Lisa
Nikola	Lisa's Co-worker in Montreal who translated Anelia's letter
Olga	Lisa's friend from Pleven who lives in Buffalo
Peter	Father of Lisa, Anelia, Vasil, Tanya and Blagorodna; Adopted son of Kiro & Luba; Husband of Ruska; Boyfriend of Natalie
Polina	Lisa's Buffalonian friend who has family in Plovdiv
Radoslav	Son of Aleksander; Brother of Momchil; Grandson of Tanya
Rangel	One of the two men who met Corrine at the SUNYAB; Uncle of Stefan
Rositsa	Daughter of Vasil & Ekaterina; Wife of Marco; Niece of Lisa; Mother of Tatiana; Mother of Sergey
Rumen	Son of Violeta; Great-Nephew of Lisa; Grandson of Tanya; Father of Diyana & Nedelya
Ruska	Stepmother of Lisa; Wife of Peter; Mother of Anelia, Vasil, Tanya and Blagorodna
Sergey	Son of Rositsa; Grandson of Vasil; Great-nephew of Lisa; Brother of Tatiana
Simeon	Son of Boyana; Grandson of Anelia; Father of Diyana; Brother of Boyko
Stefan	Nephew of Rangel who visited SUNYAB
Stoyan	Son of Alexi & Lila; Brother of Mitko

Stoyko	Son of Janeta; Grandson of Blagorodna; Father of Tosho; Husband of Mariela; Great-nephew of Lisa
Tanya	Wife of Borislav; Daughter of Peter; Sister of Lisa; Mother of Violeta and Aleksander; Mother-in-law of Elena
Tatiana	Daughter of Rositsa; Sister of Sergey; Great-niece of Lisa
Tosho	Son of Stoyko; Grandson of Janeta; Great-great-nephew of Lisa
Valentin	Son of Boyko; Brother of Angel; Great-great-nephew of Lisa
Vasil	Son of Peter; Brother of Lisa; Father of Rositsa; Husband of Ekaterina; Grandfather of Tatiana & Sergey
Vessela	Aunt of Peter; Sister of Grandpa Kiro
Violeta	Niece of Lisa; Daughter of Tanya; Sister of Aleksander; Mother of Rumen; Grandmother of Diyana & Nedelya

Disclaimer: The events described in this memoir are based on a true story, but the names and identifying details have been changed to protect the privacy of individuals. Any resemblance to a real name is coincidental.

Appendix C

[Avramov] Family Tree

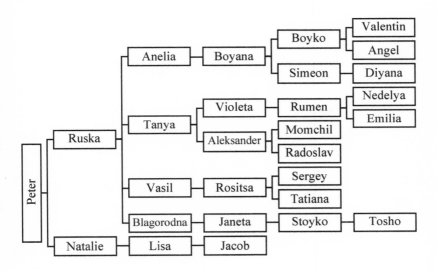

Four Generations from [Peter] to the current generation.

Appendix D

Websites and Links

Official Bulgarian tourist website
http://bulgariatravel.org/en/object/19/asenova_krepost

Green Life Family Apartments
Green Life Family Apartments

Reviews of Bulgarche Restaurant
Bulgarche

Devil's Bridge by 3 Minute Bulgaria
Devil's Bridge

Movie trailer *Live Chimneys* filmed in Kovachevitsa
Live Chimneys

Village of Leshten
http://bulgariatravel.org/en/object/301/selo_Leshten

Beautiful YouTube video of the lake at Golyam Beglik
https://youtu.be/47sRKPSgn3Q

History of Roman Plovdiv
http://www.romanplovdiv.org/

3 Minute Bulgaria video of *Boyana Church and Vitosha Mountains*
Boyana Church and Vitosha Mountains

Free Sofia Tour
http://freesofiatour.com/

Square of Tolerance
https://www.myguidebulgaria.com/attractions/the-square-of-tolerance

Hristo Hristov
  http://www.desebg.com/

The book *Former People* by Hristo Hristov and Prof. Villi Lilkov
  http://desebg.com/knigi/3167-2017-05-15-15-47-39

The film *The World is Big and Salvation Lurks Around the Corner*
      https://en.wikipedia.org/wiki/The_World_Is_Big_and_Salv
ation_Lurks_Around_the_Corner

In 2016, Rositsa shared a song by Poli Genova who represented Bulgaria in the Eurovision Song Contest with *If Love Was A Crime*. The song made us both so proud of Bulgaria. It made me cry because I felt its words portrayed dad who 'did the time' because 'love was his crime'-the love of a family.

A song called *Ya kazhi mi, oblache, le byalo* based on a poem by Ran Bosilek about an immigrant that touched my Bulgarian friends by Dessy Dobreva Oblache, le byalo

While writing this book, I found a Wikipedia article about my father and his friend, [Alexi]. The article mentions a book by Nedyalko Geshev which was written in Belgium in 1983 entitled *Belene - The Island of the Forgotten*
    https://en.wikipedia.org/wiki/Belene_labour_camp

If you need help structuring or writing your own memoir, you might contact Natasha Fernando
  thebarnicles1@gmail.com

Natasha is the founder of the B.A.R.N. Chronicles
  www.thebarnicles.org

If you need an English – Bulgarian or Bulgarian – English translator, contact Mariya Nikolova at mikence90@gmail.com

ABOUT THE COVER PHOTO AND TITLE

The cover photo for this book was taken while walking to a restaurant in Sofia at the end of my trip. At the time, I did not know what street I was on or why I took the photo except that I love old and new architecture. The striking shiny red tile against the tan building caught my eye. While searching for the perfect artwork for my cover, I remembered this photo and thought it would be perfect for the story. It symbolized more than I knew.

The building seems like just an ordinary building in a regular neighborhood. Just as my dad was an ordinary man from an unknown village. The more I admired it, the more details I could associate with it. The beige and peeling building represents the old world or Bulgaria while the shiny building represents the new world or the United States of America.

The striking bold red color stands for many things: Communism and the blood of Jesus Christ considering the Christian theme of my book. The fruits and flowers that my father cultivated in the story such as roses, geraniums, apples, strawberries and cherries are red in color. Although the old building is in Bulgaria, its three-story architecture reminded me of the apartment where I lived with my father in Buffalo. Both buildings abutted together symbolizes the fusion of the United States of America working together with Bulgaria to remember the past in order to improve the future. The old building reflecting into the new building can be seen as the older generation such as my own reflecting our hopes, dreams and values into our own children, the younger generation. Lastly, at least three crosses can be seen with the largest in the center of the photo symbolizing Christ Jesus' resurrection.

I believe that it was a result of His work on the cross that restores and redeems my own family's heritage.

The title "Red Is for Roses" is simply meant to convey that red is the best color to symbolize Bulgaria's roses and its' rich rose oil production. It was never meant to be overshadowed by the implication that red represents Communism.

INDEX

ABOUT THE AUTHORS

Lisa Ann Varco (f/k/a Lisa Ann Perinchev)

Lisa was born in 1967 in Buffalo, New York.
After graduating from high school in her hometown,
she studied Business Administration at
Erie Community College – City Campus and
The School of Management at the
State University of New York at Buffalo (SUNYAB).
She has worked in various roles as a Project Controls
Specialist and Program Scheduler in the Consulting Engineering
and Space and Defense industries.
She resides with her husband and son in Buffalo, New York.
This is her first publication.

Vanya Nikolova Pirincheva-Toteva

Vanya was born in 1960 in Plovdiv, Bulgaria.
After graduating from high school in her hometown, she studied
librarianship and bibliography at the State Library Institute
(now the University of Library Studies) in Sofia.
She has worked as a librarian in the
Processing Department and Catalogs of the
Ivan Vazov National Library in Plovdiv (1986 - 2016).
Since 2016, she has been the Head of the Library Center
at the European Higher School of
Economics and Management - Plovdiv.
Her first publication was a short text about Radoy Ralin in the
Bibleswave magazine in 1990, followed by episodic essays in
regional media and more on social networks.

Both Vanya and Lisa are devoted to their families and friends.
They enjoy reading, writing and traveling.
They are avid gardeners and cooks.

Read about the authors at:

redisforroses.com

You may e-mail them at:

Lisa@redisforroses.com

They would enjoy hearing from you.

The End

CPSIA information can be obtained
at www.ICGtesting.com
Printed in the USA
FSHW022340110819
60929FS